Ralph Milton

Through rose-colored bifocals

AN HILARIOUS CELEBRATION OF LIFE, LOVE AND FAITH

This book is dedicated to the people of
Lake Country
(Winfield, Oyama and Okanagan Centre)
with
love and gratitude.

WOOD LAKE BOOKS
Winfield, B.C.

ISBN   0-919599-13-3

Canadian Cataloguing in Publication Data

Milton, Ralph.
    Through rose-colored bifocals

        ISBN 0-919599-13-3

        1. Middle aged men - Anecdotes, facetiae,
    satire, etc. 2. Middle age - Anecdotes,
    facetiae, satire, etc. 3. Canadian wit and
    humor (English)* I. Title.
    PN6231.M47M54 1983   C818'.5407   C83-091490-0

DEAREST READER PLEASE NOTE:

We made this book as cheaply as possible, to keep the
price as low as possible, so that you could buy copies
for all your friends, and even a few of your enemies.

Printed by:
Friesen Printers
Altona, Manitoba

Wood Lake Books, Inc.,
S-6, C-9, RR 1,
Winfield, BC, V0H 2C0

Contents

Foreword
Read at your own risk   5

I Through Rose-colored Bifocals   11
    Middle deep in a mid-life crisis
    Unflappable father
    Tell me doc. How long have I got?
    Milk on my toast
    A meditation on Father's Day
    What are you teaching my daughter?
    A heavenly wish for Mrs. McNish
    Mother's strong arms

II Garbage Soup and other Culinary Delights   27
    The empty nest syndrome
    More with less
    Now do you understand, Mom?
    Heat your home for $5.00 a year
    Meditations in the throne room
    Crunchy Granola
    The day of the cow
    How much is a cubic cup?
    Here comes Peter Cottontail

II Life with the Rev   49
    Me and the Rev
    Where do babies come from?
    Faking it
    Kissing a dirty ashtray
    Flip, tug and pat

III A Man's a Man for A' That   59
    I'm proud of my nose
    At last! A cure for the common cold
    Relativity and the art of skiing
    Sweep turkey!
    The natural look in monks
    A pain in the neck

IV God Laughs Too!   71
    When I grow up
    The distant sound of laughter
    Say something in Cobol
    The ghost of Christmas past

4

V The World Traveller 80
Just in time. Just.
    So far from Toronto
    It never snows in Vancouver
    Bombs and gifts

VI Down Home 89
Tea on tap
    The blessings of an Okanagan summer
    The fine art of small talk
    Stark naked on a tractor
    Too good for TV

VI The Wonderful World of Weeds 98
The joy of gardening
    The crabgrass headache remedy
    What kind of bull is this?
    How to succeed at gardening
    The law of the jungle
    Apple picking for beginners
    Carrots are only human

A parting shot:
    A funny faith 112

Read at your own risk

This book is supposed to help you laugh.

Through it, I want to laugh with you, even though in my life, and perhaps in yours, there's been a heavy dose of personal tragedy lately. A glance at the news-media, and we know the world is in a sad state. It often seems there's nothing to laugh about.

You could call it "fiddling while Rome burns."

Putting time and effort into a book of humor while the nation's economy is shuddering, third world people are getting poorer, the atomic powers are greasing the slide to the last war of all, and we are grieving over the loss of people we love... well, the kindest thing you could call it would be "irresponsible."

And yet...

I remember a church service, years ago. The ushers had just taken up the offering. They were walking down the aisle when one of them tripped on the pile in the carpet, and sent his offering plates and those of his partner flying in a flurry of envelopes, dollar bills and quarters all over the front of the church.

The congregation sat in stunned silence.

Then the minister said the only thing that could be said. "For goodness sake, laugh."

And they did.

Till the tears rolled down their faces. And while they laughed, they got down on their hands and knees and picked up the money, put it back on the offering plates, and carried on with the worship service.

The world has always been in trouble. It may be in more trouble now than usual, but trouble is not a new thing for the human species.

There are at least two ways to react.

One way is to be so solemn about everything that you never laugh at all. It makes good sense, which is why the early Quakers tried it. "Life is tragic," they said, "therefore nobody will laugh." It's a reasonable response.

The other position is to laugh at almost everything, on the theory that the laughing, while it doesn't solve the problem, does at least put it into perspective. It's a bit like praying.

Last summer, I held a very close friend in my arms as he sobbed at the news that his son was dying. Over the months that followed, we grieved together, he for a son and I for a friend.

My friend's grief was deep and terrible. But sometimes in the grieving we'd remember his son's delightful humor, his penetrating wit, and my friend and I could laugh a little through our anger and our tears.

We didn't laugh to deny the magnitude of grief. We didn't laugh to avoid the pain. We laughed, because not to do so would have denied the beauty and the joy of a young man we loved. It would have denied the loss we were grieving.

I've said it so often, my friends are getting tired of hearing me. <u>Laughter is not the opposite of seriousness. Laughter is the opposite of despair.</u>

One of the common traits of dictators, revolutionaries, church bureaucrats and television evangelists, is that they are afraid to laugh at themselves. Laughter might reveal their humanity and uncover their nakedness.

Suppose the leaders of the world's super-powers could see how silly they really looked, standing up there like school boys shaking their nuclear fists at each other. Suppose it dawned on them that the emperor has no clothes.

Of course we must rage and protest at the danger and the injustice. Of course we must work and study and pray. But the moment we stop seeing ourselves as "fools for Christ" we lose the spark of grace so beautifully portrayed in Willis Wheatley's drawing of a laughing Jesus. He called that picture, of a man with his head back in hearty laughter, "Jesus Christ, Liberator."

We're so used to seeing Jesus portrayed as terribly solemn. I don't think he was.

Serious maybe. But serious is different from solemn.

Being serious is hard work. Being solemn is easy.

Jesus told us that to enter the "kingdom" we had to be like little children. William Barclay in his commentary on the book of Mark says children loved to hang around Jesus. Children hardly ever hang around someone who is solemn all the time.

Children are naturally serious, but they are hardly ever solemn. They undertake life with intensity and passion, and involve themselves totally in whatever is happening to themselves or those around them. That involves laughing and crying and feeling anger and love and joy and sadness.

But they hardly ever put on the adult mask of solemnity which turns out to be a very sophisticated way of ducking reality.

Humor is very serious. But it is hardly ever solemn.

True humor, says J.B. Priestley in his book English Humour, is not the same as that which is merely laughable. It has a number of ingredients. There's a feeling for irony, "a sense of the absurd; a certain contact with reality, one foot at least on the ground; and, perhaps at first sight surprising, affection."

Humor has more to do with attitude than with laughter. We've lost that understanding, because we've allowed humor to be defined for us, first of all by the music-hall stage, then by situation comedies on television where humor often consists simply of verbal violence.

Violence is pornographic. It is very solemn, and never funny.

Humor rather should be defined by people like Tevya in the musical Fiddler on the Roof. When the peasant Jews are being expelled from their homes in Russia, one villager says, "Anatevka hasn't been exactly the Garden of Eden." The Rabbi observes that their people "have been forced out of many places at a moment's notice."

"Maybe," quips Tevya, "that's why we always wear our hats."

Maybe that's why Jewish people are still around to tell their stories. "Tears dipped in honey," a friend once called it.

Jesus was a Jew who lived when times were at least as bad as they are now. He used wild hyperbole and wry humor, as much as he used cries of outrage to confront the powers and principalities.

Leo Tolstoy, a great Christian who also lived in a time of turmoil, put it this way:

"If someone were to tell me that it lay in my power to write a novel explaining every social question from a particular viewpoint that I believed to be the correct one, I still wouldn't spend two hours on it. But if I were told that what I am writing will be read...by the children of today, and that those children will laugh, weep and learn to love life as they read, why then I would devote the whole of my life and energy to it."

Tolstoy I am not. But the gift of humor is sometimes mine. And if the articles that follow in this book help a few of us to "laugh, weep and learn to love life" while we confront the evil that threatens our world; why then that is reason enough for writing them.

That, anyway, is the theological and philosophical rationale for writing this book. Every serious book has to have that kind of rationale. Why shouldn't a funny book?

But let's not kid ourselves. It does not really explain or justify it. You can arrive at your own conclusions.

All of what follows had its real beginnings in a restaurant on the MacLeod Trail in Calgary where they serve stale egg rolls. We (Bev, to whom I've been married for a quarter of a century, and I) referred to it affectionately as the Salmonella Inn.

Bev had just come back from Naramata, a church leadership training center in the Okanagan Valley of B.C. She'd been at a seminar of some sort. And she wanted some Chinese food.

When Bev is pregnant, with a child or with a new idea, she wants Chinese food. I knew she wasn't expecting a baby, because I'd had a vasectomy and she'd had a hysterectomy and a real pregnancy would have been at least a medical miracle. It had to be an idea she was gestating.

"I discovered I want two things," she said half way through the stale egg roll. "I want a full-time church and I want to move back to the mountains."

Bev is a Rev; an ordained minister. Up till that

time she had been pastoring part-time at Red Deer Lake, a small congregation just south of Calgary.

I was a TV producer. Not a big name doing network super-specials, but I was doing all right. Except that I was working harder and harder and enjoying it less and less. And I was remembering that at the age of 13 I had decided to be a writer when I grew up. It was time to grow up.

A call had come for her to become the pastor of a church in Winfield, just north of Kelowna in B.C.'s beautiful Okanagan Valley. It took a fair bit of doing to rearrange our lives so that Bev was the wage earner and I did the cooking. It wasn't that I objected to being full-time house husband and part-time writer. I just didn't know how.

Soon after we arrived in Winfield, I discovered a long-lost second cousin named Jack McCarthy. He was running the local weekly newspaper. He got me started writing a weekly "humor" column.

I have this strong tape in my head that says once you've made a commitment you stick to it. So I had to write those columns even when I didn't feel like it. Often I had to push myself to see the irony, the absurd and the beautiful in the things that were happening to Bev and me and our kids. And that made it possible to write both laughingly and lovingly about us and about the many friends who adopted us in what turned out to be a very warm and friendly community and a lively, vital and caring church.

We find ourselves living in what Alvin Toffler calls the "electronic cottage". The telephone, the post office, the airplane, along with a VW Rabbit named God-iva (she's white all over and without accessories) and a small computer named Wolfgang, (what else could you call a computer?) make it possible for me to have the best (and some of the worst) of both the urban and rur-al worlds. That meant I could type some words into Wolf-gang, give him a few instructions, then step outside and pick parsnips while he did the dirty work.

Bev and I thought some of these columns might help some of you laugh your way over a few minor bumps and scrapes; to be more serious about life, but not quite so solemn.

Not everything in this book will make you laugh. But I hope there are not too many places where I've lost the grace of humor.

Every one of of the articles in this book is based on a real incident. But sometimes I exaggerate just a teensy bit. And I have a weird mind that goes off in strange directions. There is fair bit of what Pooh-Bah called "corroborative detail designed to add artistic versimilitude to an otherwise dull and unconvincing narrative."

So the names, places and especially the facts have been changed, not to protect anyone, but because I could never really get them straight anyway.

Read at your own risk.

I

Through rose-colored bifocals

Middle deep in a mid-life crisis

Here in Winfield I am known chiefly as "the minister's husband". She is known as "Rev Bev". She earns the family income. Whatever I bring in with my writing and book publishing covers peanut butter and other "extras".

That's a big change from the way things used to be. Bev and I have had to work out a whole new set of relationships, and that was not at all easy. It was a new kind of "growing up," that was probably more difficult than the first.

To complicate the whole thing, both of us were going through a very real period in our lives that is called "the mid-life crisis." It's not unlike being a teenager all over again. You face many of the same questions, and the same uncertainties gnaw at your insides.

Suddenly the older generation isn't "them" anymore, it's "us". You become aware of your own mortality as heart disease and cancer seem to hit more and more people. My mother died, which for me was both a terrifying and a very beautiful event.

Mid-life can be a good time if you let it because life takes on a quality and a richness it didn't have before. And at least some of your priorities get straightened around.

There are new feelings to be dealt with. Some of them are fun. For instance, I had to learn to cook. Well sort of. You might get a second opinion from Bev and the kids. But the feelings of pride when you bake your first real tuna casserole and the sense of failure when you bring in the "burnt offerings" are not to be minimized.

I'll long treasure the satisfaction of being asked by one of the ladies at a church supper for the recipe for my salad dressing, even though I eventually had to admit it came out of a bottle.

There are other, more important feelings. Bev gets

invited to go to various events and functions, because in a real sense she is a community minister in this town. And I get invited along because I am her husband. Sometimes I feel like Prince Philip walking half a step behind the Queen.

Bev knows what that's like. For years, she came along as "the good wife" to events where I was the "star". For the first 15 years of our life together, neither of us gave it a second thought.

Now the shoe is on the other foot, and I'm beginning to understand why many women are so deeply angry and hurt about the role society has assigned them.

In the middle of all this, our kids suddenly grew up. I was just getting used to thinking of them as teenagers when I looked up from the evening paper and saw they were leaving home. For years we fought over who got into the bathroom next. Now you can walk right in without even taking a number. I don't even have to check to make sure I have something on.

As anyone who has been through it knows, being parent to teenagers is an awesome education. There is a bittersweet pain as you watch them grow too fast into a world that is cold and cruel and sometimes wonderful. I want to pull them back toward me, even as I'm nudging them out of the nest. I ache for them to come home again, yet I'm proud to see them standing on their own.

It's hard to learn to let go. Perhaps that's all part of growing up. My growing up. Not theirs.

Unflappable father

There are some things you never forget. Like the day my children turned into teenagers. I knew the moment it happened. They let me have the prize in the cereal box.

Being an intelligent concerned father, I was naturally a little, ah, shaken. I spoke to Bev about it. She just patted me on the shoulder and smiled.

Then there was the day I tried to phone home. We were still living in Calgary where I had a real office with a secretary who smiled at everyone. I wanted to know what it was I was supposed to remember to do. The line was busy.

I tried again at five minute intervals, then ten. I kept trying till 4:25 when I finally got through.

A man answered!

"I'm sorry," I said politely. "I must have the wrong number."

"No you don't, Dad. It's me."

Being a cool unflappable father, I controlled the quaver in my voice and said with full parental authority, "I'd like to speak to your mother."

"Hi," Bev said. "What's up?"

"What's up?" I lost control of the quaver. "I've been trying to get through for hours. Who have you been talking to?"

"Me?" she said. "It's those daughters of yours." (Funny how they always get to be my kids when there's something wrong.)

"But that's impossible!" I sputtered. "Who would they be talking to?"

"Boys!"

"Boys? They don't know any boys!"

"C'mon, Ralph," she said. "Where have you been?" That did it. I decided it was time to assert my masculine authority.

"Now look here, woman. I've been at this office, working my fingers to the bone to earn a decent living for you people. Then I phone home and the line is busy, busy, busy, and when I finally get through some man answers the phone who pretends to be my son, and you have the nerve to ask me where I've been!"

"Come home as soon as you can, dear. We'll sit down after supper and talk about it." She hung up.

"Obviously," I said to myself, "obviously I am needed at home. Something is going on, and it needs the firm steady hand of a male."

I was right. I walked in the door and there next to the stereo, wearing earphones, one of my daughters was having a seizure. Her body was contorting into the most horrendous positions. From her lips came the wail of a starving wolverine; her eyes were glazed and unseeing.

"Quick honey! Come here," I called to Bev. "Look at your daughter. She's possessed!"

It was my wife's turn to have a seizure. I think she was laughing. But she may have been crying, or a little of both.

"Ooh, Ralph," she wailed. "Your daughter is listening to Elton John, and she sings and dances while she listens on the earphones."

I don't remember much of what happened over supper, except that it seemed awfully noisy. But later, sitting beside my wife on the sofa, when all four youngsters were in their rooms, each of them listening to a different radio station, I remembered what I wasn't supposed to forget.

"But why should I go buy a book called How to Understand Your Teenager? Look Bev," I said with fatherly firmness, "I was a teenager once. I don't need to read any books about it!"

Tell me doc.
How long have I got?

My dear adoring daughter cast her limpid gaze upon me. "You know, Dad," she said, "you'll look very distinguished when your hair has finished turning gray."

I began to wonder. Could I be getting on? Is it possible I'm not as young as I used to be? Quickly I checked my pulse. I couldn't find it! In a mild panic I phoned my friendly, neighborhood medic.

"Just give me the 10,000 mile checkup," I said very casually as I strolled into his office.

"You mean the 16,000 kilometre checkup," he corrected. Needless to say, between my doctor and myself there is a generation gap.

"Listen," I said. "The model you're looking at still runs on miles and gallons and yards and feet. This is a vintage body. A collector's item. They don't make our kind any more."

He wasn't impressed. "Take your clothes off," he said laconically. Poking at the dear departed muscle in my middle he asked all sorts of personal and embarrassing questions. "How much exercise are you getting?"

"Well, I do manage to get up in the morning and drag myself to the breakfast table," I said. "And I do get to the table for lunch and also for supper. I even manage a bedtime snack most evenings. And I get a good workout jumping to conclusions."

He was under-whelmed.

Then he went to the deep-freeze and got out that little gadget with the tubes on the end that he sticks in his ears, and then plants the cold steel disc right on the place where your heart, until that moment, was beating. He listened in one place, then another and another, and even tried my back in half a dozen places. I assume he heard something eventually, because when he told me to lie down on that rock-hard excuse for a bed, he didn't cover my face with a sheet.

"Have any trouble sleeping?"

"Well, I don't have trouble mornings. I usually have a nap before lunch. And I have a good nap in the middle of the afternoon. And I mostly fall asleep reading the paper after supper. But when I get to bed I often have a real problem getting to sleep."

He poked and prodded a few more places. "Does this hurt?"

"No, it tickles," I said, writhing in agony.

Finally he stopped. Or maybe he gave up. "I have some bad news for you."

I braced myself. "Yes?"

"You're got an incurable disease."

"My God! What is it?"

"Life."

"Is it serious."

"Serious? It's terminal!"

At first I was going to laugh, but I wasn't sure he was being funny. "Is that all?"

"What else do you want?"

At home again, I looked in the mirror. "What else could I want?" I said to myself. "And yes, I will look very distinguished when I finish going gray."

If I don't go bald first.

Milk on my toast

Have you been keeping up with scien-
tific research lately? I have. I
read all the major scholarly jour-
nals, like Reader's Digest, T.V.
Guide as well as Redbook.

One of the things the scientists have been saying lately is
that the mind and body are all part
of the same thing. Now anybody who
knows anything could have told them
that, but scientists have to
prove everything before they can
believe anything.

(I actually saw a research
paper done by a student at Columbia
University in New York which proved
that children, when they have been
disciplined by a parent, sometimes
feel anger towards that parent.)

Since it's now official that mind and body are all
part of the same human person, I hope they will get on
to discovering a cure for a favorite problem of mine.
It has something to do with the mind and body not getting their act together. It goes like this.

Why is it that half way through the process of doing something I forget what it is that I'm doing?

For instance, I will go from the bedroom to the
kitchen to get something. By the time I get to the kitchen I forget what it is I went there for, and then
stand there in the middle of the kitchen with a silly
look on my face.

It's worse when I have to go and get a hammer or a
pair of pliers to fix something in the house. My tools
are in a building out in the back yard. In winter I
struggle into boots and jacket, hike all the way out
there and stand in the freezing cold wondering what I
came for.

So I take a wild guess and come back with a screw-
driver or an oil can. And Bev gives me a strange look
because she knows I wanted to pull a nail.

There have been times when I was driving somewhere
in the car, and it seemed to drive itself while my mind

was busy arguing with the sermon I heard last Sunday,
and suddenly I wind up back home and that isn't where I
intended to go at all. At least not until I had been
wherever it was I was going.

My friends call it premature senility, but it's
not true. I've been that way ever since I was a kid.
The problem is the way my mind is organized.

Some people's minds are organized like a computer,
with everything exactly where they put it.

My mind is organized like my daughter's bedroom.
It's all there, and it's very interesting, but you
never really know where anything is when you want it.
And you often find things you'd rather not, at least
right at that moment.

Once, on an airplane, I got into a conversation
with a very serious veterinarian from Trochu, Alberta.
He was telling me in more detail than I really wanted,
how to find out if cows are pregnant.

"You have to shove your hand in up to your elbow
and see if you can feel the calf", he said solemnly. "I
sometimes do several hundred cows a day."

It all started to strike me as very funny, the
image of this man thrusting his arm in and out of the
south end of cows. Then I started giggling because it
occurred to me that a cow which had lost its calf would
be "decaffeinated". Get it? "De-calf..." Never mind.

But you see what I mean?

My problem is not all that terribly serious, I suppose. And it probably won't get much attention from
the psychiatrists and biologists working on the connec-
tions between mind and body. They have better things to
do, like discovering a cure for terminal acne.

So far my illness isn't too incapacitating. But
it's getting worse.

This morning I poured milk on my toast.

A meditation on Fathers' Day

Fathers' Day is that day in June when I remember that I
haven't yet paid the bills for Mothers' Day.

I bought Bev a very nice gift last Mother's Day.
I got the idea from a big ad in one of those junk mail
pieces that clutter our postboxes. It said, "just what

mother would choose for herself!" They were selling fertilizer and weedkiller.

"Who am I to argue with a piece of junk mail?" I
said. So I bought her two 10 kg. bags of stuff that's
supposed to fertilize the grass and kill the weeds.
She said, "Gee thanks!" but didn't sound very enthusiastic. Anyway, my weeds are doing fine and the grass is
turning yellow, which I'm sure is just what she wanted
for Mother's Day.

Father's Day is a very important event that should
be soberly observed in every home that has one.
Fathers are a convenience feature almost as useful as
an automatic dishwasher. Kids, for example, find them
as useful for dispensing money as those contraptions at
the bank where you can get money at 2 in the morning.
And the only code-word the kids have to remember is
"Please".

As fathers, we hold up the ideals we want our kids
to live up to. We want them to have all the things we
never had ourselves. Like "A's" on report cards. And
we spend a lot of time doing the kids' homework while
they are busy watching television.

Whatever time we have left, we spend trying to
keep the wolf from the door and from our daughters.
When we're not doing that, we're trying to give our
kids good advice, which is almost as much of a waste of
breath as playing a saxophone.

Sooner or later the kids learn how to be good sons
and daughters, but not until they become parents themselves. By the time a man realizes that his father was
usually right he has a son who thinks he's usually
wrong. In fact, it never occurs to a boy of eighteen
that some day he'll be as dumb as his Dad.

We had an expectant father visiting us last week.
There's nobody more helpless than an expectant father.
This chap told me he was going to prenatal classes.
They even taught him how to breathe during labor. He
seemed a little unclear as to who was actually going to
have the baby.

Maybe I'm a touch jealous, because when I was having babies, everyone ignored me. Bev got all the attention. Which may have been just as well, because it
seems to me all this prenatal training for fathers mostly gets them so hyper that by the time the baby is born
they collapse in a pile of sweaty jelly on the delivery
room floor.

This man's expectant wife was with him, but she

wasn't having any problems. She acted as if the whole thing was normal.

When expectant fathers (and mothers) are working on child-wonder No. 1, they read all the books and magazines and really understand all the mistakes their parents and friends made with their children, which they will certainly not make themselves.

But somewhere between the fourth and the seventeenth year, when the child starts raising hackles in the neighborhood, fathers stop believing in heredity. And they stop giving advice to other fathers.

It slowly dawns on them that at five years old your child is your master, at ten your slave, at fifteen your double, and after that either friend or foe, depending on whether they think Dad will "lend" them five dollars.

Never mind. Somewhere along the line we realize there should have been a test to check our qualifications for fatherhood, and that probably we would have all flunked.

Our fundamental defect is that we want our kids to be a credit to us. Our parents didn't manage that, and there's no reason we should expect it.

All we can do is try to live like the Dads our kids thought we were, before they became teenagers.

What are you teaching my daughter in school?

Parents should worry about their kids. That's one of the major functions a parent has. The more you worry, the better you are at parenting.

That's why I'm worrying about what they're teaching my eldest daughter in the big city of Kelowna. She's in a biology class at Okanagan College.

At first I was worried they might talk about the birds and the bees in that class until I realized she had learned about that almost before I did. What she is studying is far more frightening than birds and bees. She's learning about jeans. Or is it genes?

But even with all my parental concern, I still managed to learn a few things from her. Like, there are two kinds of genes. Dominant and recessive. Now I don't mind the dominant ones, but I've seen some of those recessive genes the girls wear in the summertime, and I don't think they should be teaching courses about that at college.

But what's even worse is the homework they give. Suddenly, around the dinner table, I found myself being researched on the subject of ear lobes. Daughter was doing a survey.

Did you know that if you have ear lobes like mine that flap about in the breeze, you have a dominant gene for ear lobes. But if they're stuck to the side of your face you are suffering from one of those no good recessive genes. The same thing if you have blue eyes like Paul Newman, or a straight nose. I have neither!

I learned something else about genes. And here I'm in trouble because it's hard to be delicate about this. You know what happens when you eat asparagus? Or beans?

For some people, there are what might be called odoriferous after-effects, if you get my meaning. That's because they have all those nice dominant genes that produce methyl mercaptan when you eat asparagus or beans. People with recessive genes can't do that, no matter how hard they try. I pity them. Poor odorless creatures.

With all of that, I decided I'd better check out my daughter's school books to see if they were suitable for her delicate eyes. I found the most shocking things. Like this sentence, for instance. "If both parents are dominant, and you exhibit the dominant phenotype too, assume yourself to be homozygous dominant." Well!!!

I mean it is certainly true that both my daughters' parents have "leadership qualities" but I don't know if I like being called "dominant". Would you?

And there is no reason she has to go around exhibiting her phenotype. It isn't nice.

And as for that homozygous business; well maybe we should call in Jerry Falwell.

Actually, I knew all this would happen the day she came home and told me they had been experimenting with fruit flies. Some of them, she said, were red-eyed mutants. Now what parent wouldn't find that shocking?

It's not as if they are studying good wholesome bugs that earn a decent living eating my cabbage. No sir. They have to study some red-eyed mutant fruit fly wearing those recessive blue genes. It's immoral. And they produce baby fruit flies every two weeks, which means they're either pretty careless or just plain shameless.

I try to do a good job of being a worrying parent. And my daughter, alone in a lab somewhere with an immoral red-eyed mutant fruit fly; well that certainly is something that should give me lots of worrying material. Enough for at least a week.

A heavenly wish for Mrs. McNish

Want to know how I got my bald spot? Or why I have this nervous twitch? Music!

The first time it happened I was walking down the hallway of a junior college. There, in one of the rooms, was a music teacher, a woman about eight feet tall in both directions. Beside her was a child no more than two feet high.

In her sweaty little hand the child had one of those Suzuki violins, about six inches long. From that small instrument she produced a squeal that loosened my dandruff and cured my fallen arches. It took three visits to the dentist to re-seat my back teeth.

But the teacher, bless her, smiled very nicely and said, "That was lovely, Susy. Now try again, but this time don't press quite so hard."

I panicked. I ran the hundred yard dash in twelve seconds flat, enough to get out of earshot, but by then I had a slight curvature of the spine and my hair was falling out. The rest of my hair fell when my own son started learning the violin. Did you know that the sound of a violin, when played just slightly sharp, can penetrate even the dark recesses of a bathroom when the water's running? And when a second son started on the

trumpet, an instrument capable of bringing water to a
boil long before the microwave was invented, I developed a nervous twitch.

All of this brings me to a very important theological issue. It seems to me, if there is any justice in
the life hereafter, surely Susy's teacher and my kids'
music instructors and all their long-suffering collea-
gues should have some special heavenly reward. They
get precious little down here.

So in case God is interested, I'd like to suggest
a room in that celestial palace where clean, well wash-
ed polite cherubs who never chew bubblegum will arrive
on time and well practised for all their lessons. And
they will play everything perfectly in tune.

And while I'm at it, may I humbly suggest a room
be reserved for us parents of music students. Hopeful-

ly in doing so, the good Lord will overlook a few unkind words and temper tantrums, considering all we've been through.

The executive suite in that pearly palace should be reserved, I'm convinced, for people like Mrs. McNish. Mrs. McNish teaches band in a junior high school; four classes of grade seven students. In each class there are forty students.

Do you have any idea, any concept, of what a grade seven student sounds like the first time he or she blows a trombone? Well, it's somewhere between the sound of an asthmatic diesel locomotive and a water buffalo with hemorrhoids.

Multiply that by forty, continue for thirty minutes and repeat four times daily. It's the fastest prescription I know of for turning a good mind into Silly Putty.

Mrs. McNish is either a person of fantastic faith or utmost imbecility. She believes, yes believes, that one day those drippy-nosed grade sevens blasting that mind-bending cacophony, those pubescent pre-teens blowing peanut butter particles into their piccolos, will one day take a chair in a great orchestra--the Berlin Symphony or even Lawrence Welk.

Music teachers of the world--here is good news! Luke, Chapter 6. "Blessed are those who weep, for they shall laugh."

Mother's strong arms

Every father is also a son. For each of us, there comes a time when you find there is no longer someone whose son you can be.

Mother had aged 10 years in 12 months. It's not that there was anything wrong, it's just that everything was wrong.

The fingers that could crochet a pair of slippers in half an hour simply wouldn't move anymore.

The heart that had laughed and cried with all the many people she loved, seemed to have developed some malfunctions. That never stopped her heart from loving, but last Saturday it stopped the heart from beating.

Mother knew death was near. But she wasn't afraid of death. It was the dying that was so painful, so frightening.

Mother and I had a long talk in the hospital a few months ago. She held my hand very tightly and asked, "You won't abandon me just because I'm so useless?"

"Of course not, Mom. How could I abandon you?"

"But I'm so useless. I can't do anything anymore. I'm not good for anything."

"Mom, I love you. Of course I won't abandon you. Neither will the rest of your family."

"But what good am I? I can't do anything except just sit here and stare at the walls."

At first I thought Mother's fear was of being abandoned by her children. But that wasn't it. She knew us better than that. Her pain was far deeper. It was the pain of our whole society that teaches us we are valued for what we can produce, by how well we can perform, by what we can achieve. It was a pain we all share.

Of course, deep down Mother knew the greater truth. Earlier we had been talking about the latest great-grandchild. It had been born on Valentine's day, and we laughed over a photograph showing a heart-shaped birthmark on its bottom.

"I guess babys can't do anything either," she said.

I knew what she meant. Babies are useless, but they are precious. Old people are useless, but they are precious. In fact all of us, when you come right down to it, are pretty useless. But we are precious. Precious I hope, to other people. Precious at least to God, who sees the sparrow fall and numbers the hairs on our head.

"Mom," I said. "Do you remember how often you told me about the time when I was just a kid, and I'd be playing out in the back yard, and every once in a while I would run into the house and I would leap up into your arms and get a quick hug, and then run right back out again?"

She held my hand a little tighter. She remembered.

"Mom, you had strong arms, and even though I'd take a flying leap at you, you'd always catch me and give me a hug."

She smiled. "I couldn't catch you in my arms anymore, Ralph."

"I know Mom. But I still come running in for a hug. Only now, you catch me with your heart."

That's why, when we gathered in a church in Winnipeg, all her family and her friends, we didn't gather to mourn, even though there was weeping. We gathered to thank God, and to celebrate the life of a woman who for 82 years was able to catch so many of us in her strong arms and hold us in her loving heart.

II

Garbage soup and other culinary delights

The empty nest syndrome

"For the love of Pete, will you label the things you put in the fridge."

That's Bev talking. She's suffering from the middle-age malady known as the Empty Nest Syndrome. It's what you get when you've been used to years of having a gaggle of hungry children underfoot. Suddenly there are no more children. They've either all left home, or grown up, or both.

At the moment, we're struggling to adjust from a household of six who ate constantly, to two or three who usually eat at mealtimes.

All of this is complicated by the fact that Bev is a Rev. She insists on preaching sermons on passages such as Genesis 1: 27-31 (look it up!) which somehow gets translated into saving all those plastic containers that come from the store.

Here the plot thickens. I used to know exactly how much spaghetti to cook for two adults and four teenagers. It was easy. You got the biggest pot you could find and filled it till the spaghetti ran out all over the stove.

The left-overs, if there were any, got put into those plastic containers. Since almost everything got eaten before the next meal anyway, there was never much congestion in the fridge.

Except for left-over zucchini.

We always found left-over zucchini in the fridge on the one day of the week when all the kids had taken their peanut butter sandwiches to school, and Bev and I would open the fridge to see what was for lunch. If Bev was working on a stewardship sermon, we ate zucchini.

Now, in spite of our best efforts to reduce quantities, we seem to fill four or five of those plastic containers with left-over spagetti. And nobody knows how many cottage cheese containers full of zucchini there are in the fridge.

Every once in a while we make a firm decision to label everything. Its really no trouble at all. Just a bit of masking tape and a felt pen.

For a week or so, full of good intentions, we stick on a hunk of masking tape, and identify the contents of every recycled plastic container that goes in

the fridge. Even the zucchini.

But then, well, resolve falters. Or we get busy. And soon the following exchange is heard.

"Ralph, where is the left-over meatloaf?"

"It's in the fridge."

"Where in the fridge?"

"In the cottage cheese container."

"Which cottage cheese container?"

"The one marked 'zucchini'."

There is a long pause, then: "There are eight cottage cheese containers marked 'zucchini'." I hear an edge of hysteria in her voice.

"It's in the blue cottage cheese container marked 'zucchini' with the yellow margarine lid marked 'ketchup'."

There's another way of knowing when you have the Empty Nest Syndrome--when you leave a chocolate cake on the table, and it's still there twenty minutes later.

More with less

Don't ever give anyone the More with Less Cookbook. Somebody did that to us once, and we haven't had a moment's peace since.

The book, which comes out of the Mennonite tradition I share with Doris Janzen Longacre, makes two very convincing points.

Too much of the paraphenalia of contemporary living keeps you from getting into real contact with your family, your friends, yourself and your God.

Simplify. Stop running around like a headless chicken and take a bit of time to find out how plants and children grow. Stand still so people can hug you.

The other point Longacre makes is that "consumerism" isn't fair. When half the world goes to bed hungry, it just isn't right, it isn't just, for us to be stuffing ourselves. Whether we can afford it or not is beside the point.

She's right of course. I wish she wasn't.

I have my own evidence to support her argument. I had all sorts of trouble with hyper-acid stomach and tension headaches. I'm a chronic workaholic. That means I have to struggle hard at living a more balanced life, a life that values people. Including myself.

Our conversion from consumerism came less as a matter of conviction and more as a matter of necessity. Bev was brand new in the ordained ministry, serving a small congregation, which meant she was at the bottom of the salary scale. It's a survival salary designed for very young, small families. We have four kids in college.

So, we planted a dozen fruit trees in our yard and trucked manure and other compost onto a garden where the soil was better suited to making pots than planting vegetables. And we harvested and preserved, and dried and pickled, and generally tried to live more with less.

We began patronizing the "Thrift Shop", a second-hand store our congregation runs in order to recyle used goods and to raise money for missions and other good work. It's amazing the things you can get if you keep your eyes open.

And "a penny saved is a penny earned" as it says in the good book. (The Farmer's Almanac.)

A wood stove was next.

It was fun, although we soon found we had to temper our enthusiasm. I still have the can of lye for the soap which we never made. There simply isn't time for some things.

And now that our publishing business is taking off, and Bev's church is bouncing with activity, we find ourselves with two full time jobs and nobody to wash the dishes. "What we need around here is a wife," Bev keeps muttering.

We keep working at the more with less ideals. Not so much now because of the money it saves, but because of the more balanced life it offers; physical health and the sense of wholeness. Most of the time we're only a little bit successful. At least we've discovered that sometimes leading a "balanced" life may mean not undertaking some money or resource saving work.

Bev keeps preaching sermons about Christian lifestyles and world justice. We have to at least try to practise what she preaches.

(Sometimes I wish she'd preach some nice pious little sermons, like the ones on TV. A massage, not a message; sermons that make you feel warm all over but never challenge you to change anything.)

So if you've got a good thing going in utter suburbia, complete with conspicuous over-spending and commuter blues, hang on to it. Don't ever buy the More with Less books.

Unless you're looking for trouble.

Now do you understand, Mom?

The way to save money and be a good Christian is to heat your house with wood. Wood is a renewable resource, so it's good ecology. It's cheaper, good exercise, and gives you a sense of being one with nature.

That's so nice to know. And, as our cosy family nestles around the cheerfully crackling fire on a cold winter eve, drinking hot chocolate and talking about how wonderful everybody and everything is, it helps me not to think of what my mother said to me a year ago last spring.

We had a nice big black bulky airtight stove sitting there waiting to be installed. "You are out of your cotton-pickin' mind, sonny," mother said. Or words to that effect.

With a directness that only mothers can muster,

she told me how she used an ecologically sound, wood burning cookstove for more years than she cared to remember, and that they were dirty, smelly, and back-breaking.

But small boys, even when they are middle-aged small boys, always know better than their mothers. So I paid the price of ten years electric heating to have a chimney and the stove installed. Add the price of a chain saw, gas to haul the wood home and linament for my aging muscles, and I should break even in about 15 years.

According to the advertising, this wonderful air-tight stove leads a double life as a fireplace, so that it's not only good ecology, it promotes things like family life, togetherness and apple pie. You take the door off, pop a screen in place, then lie down on your bear rug to enjoy the blaze. (The bear rug is optional.)

What the advertising didn't say is that when you open the door, black billows of acrid smoke come rolling out, asphyxiating the whole household and setting off your brand new smoke alarm that is supposed to tell you when the house is burning down.

Our smoke alarm worked quite well, actually. It set off a yowl that brought everybody in our house running, hands over ears, throwing books, old shoes and sandwiches at that screaming machine.

But I, being the most cool, calm, unflappable person in the whole valley, simply climbed on a chair, ripped that wailing siren from the ceiling (leaving a hole you'd never notice in the dark) and flushed it down the toilet.

(Which is why, to this day children, if you should walk in our garden in the silence of midnight, you can hear rising from the bowels of the earth the lonely spirit of a departed smoke alarm sobbing in the slime of our cesspool.)

I am never daunted by adversity. "Let courage rise with danger, and strength to strength oppose;," as the old hymn has it. So I simply carried on with the job at hand, which was gathering wood to feed our wonderful, ecologically sound airtight stove. After only two weeks of work, I had enough wood for the next month.

That is why I am so happy. I sit here at my typewriter, my beautiful black stove crackling merrily beside me, and tears running down my cheeks.

Some cynics would say the tears are from the fumes

of linament on the sore back I got from sawing wood. Others would say it's because of the smoke in the air. Still others would opine that I had caught a cold from the draft of a door left open to clear the smoke.

All are wrong.

These are tears of sheer and utter joy, as I think about all the benefits wood heat brings to my family; the expression of delight on the face of my son when I asked him to chop and pile the wood, the friendly buzz of the vacuum cleaner as it sucks up the thick layer of dust that collects on everything, and the thought that I am doing my bit to make this a better world in which to live.

Now do you understand, Mom?

Heat your home for $5.00 a year

The answer to high heating costs is in your mailbox. For as little as $5.00 a year, you can have a whole winter's fuel supply delivered to your front door, courtesy of our faithful Post Office.

The answer, of course, is junk mail. Those of us ecologically minded souls who sweated and fussed out in the bush cutting down standing dead wood, who hauled it and bucked it and split it in our backyards, and who used up as much energy doing it as we'll get from the wood itself, can now warm our tootsies in front of a roaring fire that comes to us from those same forests, only by a longer route.

Think of it this way. For a small investment of $5.00 you can hire the best loggers in the land to cut down our finest timbers, denude our forests, strip the land and leave it desolate. That same fiver will get you a smoking factory to mash it into pulp, and press it into paper. Finally, as a bonus, you get printers who smear it with multi-coloured ink, that'll translate into first class acid rain when burned.

We already get lots of junk mail. It outweighs and outnumbers mail we want by 10 to 1. And the recycling depot won't take most of it anyway. "Waste not, want not!" as it says in the Bible (doesn't it?), so you've got to do something constructive with it.

That's how the five bucks comes in. Look at the cheap ad section at the back of almost any magazine. The cheaper the magazine, the better. Wherever it offers anything free, send for it. It doesn't matter what it is or whether you're interested or not. Just be sure you never sign your name to anything or you may find you've bought a life-size plastic water buffalo with pink rhinestone eyes.

So write for stuff. All it takes is a stamp, envelope and paper. And from one letter alone, you could net enough junk mail to heat your home for two weeks. From $5.00 worth of stamps, you'd get almost enough for a Saskatchewan winter.

Here's how it works. Mailing lists feed on each other. Those people out there in that funny land where they do all this direct mail peddling sell their mailing lists to each other, so not only do you get junk mail from one outfit, you will get it from half a dozen more, and more, and more.

I know this is true because it happened to this couple I know. They were getting married. Their "friends" held a party one night, and spent it writing away in the couple's name for all sorts of things they advertise in the back of cheap magazines. For years, they received more junk mail than anyone else in the whole city. They could have filled their house and backyard with "genuine imitation diamond rings" and "photographs" of Jesus that glow in the dark. And of course there were those plain brown envelopes that sizzled when you opened them.

If you send your name and address to just a few outfits like that, your junk mail will multiply like mushrooms on a manure heap. The man in the panel truck who delivers the mail on our rural route will soon have to switch to a five-ton truck, which will eventually be replaced by a semi-trailer with one of those huge cranes so he can lift those great bales of junk mail and plunk them down on my lawn. The Post Office will become our biggest growth industry, employing thousands.

Won't it be wonderful?

There's only one very minor technical problem for which I need your help. It's already tough to find a personal letter from Aunt Maude or Uncle Harry, not to mention a cheque in all that junk mail. What will we do when ....?

Never mind. We'll work it out somehow.

Meditations in the throne room

I realize I should go see my minister about problems in my marriage. But my minister is also my wife, which makes it hard for her to be totally neutral.

Besides, how would you go explaining this kind of problem. You see, Bev and I are having this continuing disagreement over the toilet paper.

She says it should be beige. Or maybe yellow. "It goes with the colour of the walls," she says. "White is so functional!"

"It has to be white," I insist, "because we don't have a sewer, we have a septic tank, and beige doesn't decompose as fast as white."

"How do you know that?"

"Do you really want to know?"

"No."

"Let's just say that you can use beige toilet paper, provided you use it in the biffy out back."

I won that round. Because I know very well that committed as Bev is to keeping life simple, she isn't that committed. Of course she doesn't know the full nature of the threat either.

Bev is a city girl who's been deprived of the exquisite memories of the old two-holer at 40 below in a Manitoba blizzard. She's never known the delight of finding two or three pages of newsprint left in old catalogue, or the hardship when you got to the shiny pages.

Nor does she know that small boys may not aim too well, leaving small bumps of ice on the edge of the seat and that porcupines and similar sharp-toothed beasties will gnaw the edge into long sharp splinters. Sharp and cold on your backside, when you've already postponed the encounter too long because it's 40 below outside, easily qualifies as a memorable experience.

Winning a battle isn't winning a war. And the subject will come up again. Because recently I saw an ad for educational toilet paper. Sooner or later she'll spot it. Bev, who was a teacher before she was a preacher, will say it's a rotten educational method. Since it's already rotten it won't bother our septic field a bit. I'll have to work hard to talk her out of that.

This educational toilet paper comes from Japan, where they simply haven't got time to while away precious moments taking care of nature's needs. Now they learn English while they do it.

The paper has Japanese words and the English equivalents. No kidding. It's no rip-off. Any dullard can learn to read and wipe. Here in Canada we could have it in English and French. One national epidemic of diarrhea and we'd all be bilingual.

(The president of the company says women will learn more English words than men because they use 75 per-cent more toilet paper. How do you suppose he found that out?)

There's more, and you don't have to go to Yokohama for this one. It's in one of the Sears catalogues. It's a combination radio and toilet paper holder that you can install right in your wall. Combined with the teaching toilet paper, this could be the breakthrough civilization has been waiting for.

Instead of sitting there pondering trifles like the threat of atomic war or how to lead a prayer meeting in a hot tub, you can listen to the top forty, all of which blends very well with other sounds heard from time to time in the bathroom.

Now the obvious next step is to combine the toilet paper and the radio with a small computer and a bit of old-fashioned player piano technology, and you could compose a few popular bilingual songs right there in your own bathroom. The computer would punch little holes in the toilet paper, which you could then feed through the radio to hear your tune.

If you don't like what you've composed, there are other things you can do with the toilet paper.

Then let it de-compose.

Crunchy granola

Everybody knows that if you are to be accepted into the Alternate Life-Styles Middle-Class Counter-Culture, also known as the A.L.S.M.C.C.C., you have to know how to make granola.

Not only that, you have to have your own personal recipe so you can argue with others how yours is a) tastier b) cheaper and c) more nutritious. The fact that it takes a full week to make is not relevant, because time is not a factor in the ecology of the A.L.S.M.C.C.C.

The A.L.S.M.C.C.C. Great Granola Movement, also known as the A.L.S.M.C.C.C.C.G.G.M. began in the 1970's when somebody read the ingredients on a cereal box and realized that the most nutritious part of the whole package was the box itself. The wax paper came in second.

Some of us found ourselves getting a little cynical about TV commercials and slick magazine adds which claimed, "One ounce of this cereal with milk provides all the vitamins and minerals your child needs for a whole day." The commercials didn't tell us that the milk brought us all the good stuff. The cereal was mostly sweetened sawdust. Junk food in disguise.

That's when somebody somewhere started rooting around and found all sorts of exotic things you could put into breakfast cereal if you made it yourself. You mixed it all up and toasted it in the oven for a couple of days. Presto! Granola! The A.L.S.M.C.C.C.C.C.G.G.M. was born!

In many instances, this new breakfast food was even edible, provided you had good teeth. Those equipped with store teeth had to let it soak for a week.

Now because I am a naturally nice guy, I am going to violate one of the basic commandments of the A.L.S.-M.C.C.C.C.C.G.G.M. and share my granola recipe with you. And I hope you realize the risk I'm taking in doing this. They still hold heresy trials in the movement. The last heretic was sentenced to three weeks in the executive suite of the Toronto Hilton.

So here's the recipe. Take a batch of rolled oats, a batch and a half of rolled barley, a handful of sunflower seeds (with hulls removed please), a smidgen of sesame seeds, and even a bit of desecrated coconut. You mix all that up with a bit of goose grease, or vegetable oil if you don't have goose grease, and put it on pans for toasting in the oven.

There are those who insist on adding a few rat hairs for authenticity, but they're purists.

Next comes the tricky part. Timing is everything. If you don't leave it in long enough, your granola comes out looking like lumpy chicken mash. If you leave it in 1/57th of a second too long, the whole business turns into instant charcoal.

Not only that, but your house fills with smoke, the smoke alarm starts wailing, your wife shoves the children out the door, the neighbors call the fire department, and you reveal the extent of your vocabulary.

Burnt granola has very limited use. I've found the most creative thing is to put it in a bucket in the

trunk of the car to use when the road is icy and you
need something to help your tires grip. Some have fed
it to the birds, but that's a foul thing to do because
they have to flap for twenty minutes before they can
get airborne again. Some people mix it with yogurt, but
others just use ordinary cement for laying bricks.

However, let's be optimistic! Of course you'll get
it out of the oven at that delightful golden brown
stage. Then let it cool.

But you're not finished. Granola at this stage
tastes like toasted horse fodder. To really make it
taste like something, you add dried fruit. Apricots,
apples, peaches, and prunes. Some people even add dried
bananas, but personally I think that's going too far.
In fact, I plan to introduce an amendment to the bylaws
indicating that bananas in granola violates the basic
ethos of the S.L.S.M.C.C.C.C.C.C.G.G.M.

Raisins are essential. Leave them out, and you've
forgotten the raison d'etre of crunchy granola.

Let it sit for a couple of days. You will wake up
one morning to a glorious feast of healthful, nutritious granola!

One thing you should never do is count the cost.
We made that mistake only once and discovered that our
healthful, nutritious granola, what with all the dried
fruit and nuts and things, cost us $1.98 a spoonful.
And that is another heresy in the movement, because
everybody knows you save money making your own granola.

Anyway, we decided to cut out all the expensive
stuff and make the El Cheapo version referred to above
which tastes like toasted horse fodder.

Now don't tell any member of the A.L.S.M.C.C.C.C.-
C.C.C.C.G.G.M. (They'll defrock me and make me trade in
my rusty Volkswagen for a brand new gas guzzling Lin-
coln.) But we've found a way to save money making our
own granola without going broke. We mix it with commer-
cial cereal. We each mix according to taste.

I like it best with about one teaspoon of granola
well stirred into a large bowlful of Fruit Loops.

At least I'm not eating junk food.

The day of the cow

It shall be remembered in our family history as "the day of the cow." And the tale will be told from generation unto generation.

We wanted to beat the system. Beef prices were sky high! I called my buddy, Mark Bedford, who was then the minister at a neighboring church. "Look," I said, "let's buy a cow from one of the ranchers near here, cut it up ourselves and save a bundle."

It took a bit of digging, but we finally found a farmer who had a cow that hadn't produced the required calf. I felt a bit bad that death and dismemberment should be the punishment for a malfunction of the ovaries. For a fleeting moment, I wondered who would raise these justice issues on behalf of cows.

Mark and I debated long hours about what to do with this cow. We thought perhaps we'd tie a rope to its neck and lead it into town. We could do the dastardly deed in our garage. I told Bev she'd get to tan the hide.

"I have no idea how to do that," she demurred.

"You chew on it till it's pliable."

She wasn't enthusiastic.

So we compromised. For a mere $40, a local butcher put our poor childless cow out of its misery, and hung her, upside down, in a cold room for two weeks. He got to keep the hide.

Mark and I brought the beast home. I had a mild hernia hefting a quarter of dead cow down the stairs, but we finally got her down to the family room where she lay in gory glory on the sagging ping-pong table.

Mark was supposed to know how to dismember this cadaver. He'd never actually done it to a cow before, but he's a hunter and had bagged a few moose. He figured a cow couldn't be that much different.

It was. It was also different from the diagram we found in an old cookbook. In fact, this cow was an anatomical freak, having bones where no self-respecting cow should have bones. We sawed through most of them. Length-wise!

The flat pieces were labeled "steak" and the big round pieces were called "roasts". Everything else was either stewing meat or ground beef.

Half way through the first quarter we were tired. At the end of the first half we were exhausted. And as we chopped and sawed, more and more of our precious beast found its way to the pile labelled "ground beef".

Late that night over our seventy-fifth cup of coffee, we listed the costs. The cost of the cow, the killing, the hanging, the mincer, the wrapping paper, the meat saw, the linament. But for some reason, we never did add up the total.

How much is a cubic cup?

I have just discovered a major cause of social dysfunction, headaches, abdominal pain, ulcers, nausea and marriage breakdown. Recipes! Those mysterious little three by five cards that women trade at teas and bazaars. They are a major threat to the health and stability of our society. They are a particular threat to "liberated" husbands trying, at age 48, to learn to cook.

For instance, yesterday I made a pie. It was my very first pie and I tried as hard as I could to get it right. How was I supposed to know that one c.c. of salt didn't stand for "cubic cup"? Maybe I should have guessed. I couldn't find any cubic cups anywhere in the house, but I figured a round cup ought to be more or less the same.

Actually, it was a beautiful looking pie. But the conversation over dessert was a bit strained. And my, the children do drink a lot of milk.

Then there was the evening last week when I was alone in the house and I decided to make some cookies. The recipe seemed simple enough. Wouldn't it stand to reason that "tbs." would stand for "tubs"? I knew that obviously it didn't stand for bath tubs or wash tubs. I mean, I'm not that dumb. But it seemed to me perfectly reasonable that it would stand for a gravy tub. So I put in two tbs. of margarine.

I followed the recipe carefully. I cut the margarine into the flour and stuff with Bev's sewing scissors, added one cubic cup of vanilla, and then I dropped the batter onto a cookie sheet. It seemed a bit senseless, and it didn't say from how high you should drop it. I figured three feet ought to be about right, though that's probably too high.

It got all over the

walls. And it wasn't entirely clear how that one great glob of dough would get to be cookies. I thought maybe it happened in the oven somehow. How was I to know?

It said to bake in a medium oven. Our oven doesn't have any "medium", just a bunch of numbers. But it does have racks that slide in at the top, bottom or middle. My logical mind concluded that obviously the top one must be high, the bottom one low, and the middle one medium. Makes sense.

So I wound the oven up to 500 degrees--since the recipe didn't specify, that seemed like a good round number--shoved the great brown blob on to the middle rack, and sat down to read the paper.

I was half-way through the want-ads when the smoke alarm went off. I raced into the kitchen. Black clouds were billowing out of the top of the oven, and a sticky brown goo was oozing out the bottom. A miniature Mt. St. Helens.

Thinking fast, I grabbed a huge brown pot that had been left soaking full of water in the sink. I opened the oven door, and threw in the water. There was a puff of smoke, the kind they do in magic shows. And then all the lights went out. There I was, alone in the dark, the smoke burning my eyes, the alarm assaulting my ear drums.

Frankly, I'd rather not go on with the rest of this story. If you don't mind, I'd just like to be by myself for a while.

But somebody ought to do something about those recipes. They're a menace!

Garbage soup

It happens in the best of families. Parents do their best to stop it, but it never works. Kids grow up in spite of our best efforts. When that happens, we're faced with what

high-priced psychiatrists often call "the empty-nest syndrome".

One of the first symptoms of the empty-nest syndrome is garbage soup. For years, you get used to the idea that there are a certain number of warm bodies at the table, and you know how much those warm bodies will consume.

In our case, the number was six. So in our house, the whole cooking system was geared for six. The problem is that these days there are only two of us around. Sometimes three. The result? Leftovers.

A bit of this and a smidgen of that. A whole fridge full. Three tablespoons of salad, one wiener, three peas, a cup and a half of mashed potatoes, a bowl of half-eaten cornflakes, and one cold hamburger. The obvious thing to do with all this is give it a decent burial in the compost heap. In our house we make garbage soup.

Here's how it's done. Somebody says, "When's supper?" That's the signal to open the fridge door and stand there staring at all the little containers of left-overs. Take a deep breath. A very deep breath. Then one by one, remove each container, open it, sniff, make a face, and put it on the kitchen counter.

Next say a short prayer. It's a good idea to ask for divine guidance, though I have long had a sense that God not only hurts with us in our pain, but also has a sense of humor and enjoys a great celestial chortle imagining the outcome of our crazy efforts. So don't count on God for too much help making garbage soup.

Next, throw it all in a pot. All of it. If it's thick and gooey, add water, unless you decide to have stew instead. In that case, just forget the water, but follow all the rest of these steps.

Heat it to the boiling point, stirring constantly. Garbage soup or stew has a tendency to burn, and burning garbage is not a welcome odor in the kitchen.

From time to time, sniff it. If you're brave, you might even taste it. If a hungry teenager comes wandering in and says "Yuk! Who died in here?" it's best to throw the whole business out and serve cheese sandwiches.

On the other hand, if the teenager says, "Hey that smells great! What is it?", then immediately assume the knowing air of an experienced chef. To avoid telling blatant lies, wave a copy of a gourmet cookbook at

them. In fact it's wise to keep a high-quality cookbook lying open on the kitchen counter, the kind that
costs $65 and doesn't have a thing in it you can afford
to cook. Mutter something about having lost the page.

When you've got the stuff to the boiling point
(assuming you got that far) you stare at the spice
cabinet for a while and wonder what in blazes could possibly enhance (or mask) the flavor of whatever it is
you just cooked.

If you still have the nerve to put it on the
table, think of a name for it. A quasi-French name:
"Le Soup de la Potpourri" isn't bad for starters.
That's especially true if you have guests.

Bev said there was a slight look of panic in my
eyes the day a guest remarked, "How interesting! I've
never seen oranges used in soup before!"

Garbage soup has other hazards. On one occasion
I'd found some left-over beets which I put through the
blender along with everything else. Things were going
fine. We were all enjoying our purple soup, and having
a delightful family conversation.

Then somebody mentioned the word "blood!".

Here comes
Peter Cottontail

It made absolutely perfect
good sense. Kari, my daughter, had been reading a se-
quel to that More With
Less Cookbook. It was called, Living More With
Less, and it said things
about about how the way we
live here in Canada affects
the standard of living in
poorer parts of the world.
This was while we still lived in the wilds of suburban
Calgary.

"It's the beef you

eat, Dad," she said. "You're driving up the price of grain so that people in Asia and Africa can't afford to buy it."

"You have to have protein in your diet to survive," I advised her in my best fatherly tones.

"In the first place, beef is probably the most expensive and wasteful form of protein you can find," she retorted. "And secondly, we only need a fraction of the protein we eat." She was starting to sound entirely too adult for my liking. "Most of protein passes right through and gets flushed down the toilet. We have the most expensive urine in the world."

That was getting much too personal. "Teenage idealism," I grumped, and headed for the kitchen to check out what was for supper. All this talk about protein was making me hungry.

Supper was macaroni and cheese.

"Whatever happened to a steak now and again, or even good old hamburger?" I wondered out loud. Bev was sitting at the kitchen table trying to figure out how to buy the week's groceries without going broke. She was looking at a flyer advertising the week's "specials" at the supermarket. There was a big "X" through the beef add. I gulped. Kari's idealism was beginning to sound a bit more practical.

"Who would have the gall to charge that much for dead cow?"

"I've just decided," said Bev. "This family has turned vegetarian."

"No way," said I firmly. "We'll raise chickens in the garage."

"Sure," she said. "A rooster crowing at five in the morning will do wonders for neighborly relations. Besides, there are zoning laws."

I wasn't about to be silenced that easily. "Well, I'll figure out something!"

And I did. I went to the library and found a book that told how you could raise all the food you needed for a family of six in a three room apartment. (It didn't say so, but you'd need a very understanding landlord and a highly co-operative family.)

It explained about hydroponic gardening, using fluorescent lights and chemicals and water to grow tomatoes and carrots and all kinds of neat stuff.

Then it explained that rabbits and chickens convert vegetable protein to animal protein far more efficiently than cows. But chickens are smelly and noisy.

Hens laying eggs in the hallway don't do much for apartment block harmony. Rabbits, on the other hand, are quiet and, it said in the book, "relatively odorless."

"Ha!" I said. "I'll raise relatively odorless rabbits in our garage. We'll never have to eat beef again."

"Don't you think we should try some first," suggested Bev.

"Why? Meat is meat."

"I think we'd be smart to try it first."

So I went to the store and bought a package of Australian rabbit. Bev got it breaded nicely so that it looked like slightly malformed chicken and presented it for dinner one night. It didn't taste anything like the wild rabbit I remembered hunting as a boy on the Manitoba prairies. This rabbit was fat and greasy.

I don't remember how we explained why it had four drum sticks and no wings. There were a few remarks about the "weird" chicken. But we got along fine until somebody remarked that the chicken tasted "funny".

"Maybe that's because of the carrots it ate," said Bev.

Kari stopped in mid chew, a strange glazed look in her eyes. She sat there for a few stunned moments as the penny dropped. Then very deliberately, she removed the remaining rabbit from her mouth, put it on her plate, and slowly got up from the table.

"You sit right down there, young lady," I yelled. "You were eating that quite happily while you thought it was chicken so you can eat it just as well knowing it's rabbit. You hear me! Sit down!"

She sat down. But she looked me squarely in the eye.

"I won't eat it, Dad," she said quietly, with a firmness and resolve I'd never heard before.

We didn't make much progress that day with third world justice and the protein problem. But Kari learned something about her own strength and convictions.

And her Dad learned a bit about being a father.

III
Life with the Rev

Me and the Rev

Bev was a shy, skinny grade three school teacher. I was a macho DJ at the local radio station.

She and I took an instant dislike to each other. She thought I was conceited. I thought she was dull.

But we hung around the edges of the same gang, and so managed to continue our dislike for several years.

Then her boyfriend went off to the west coast to study and she needed a ride to the hospital for physiotherapy on a bad disc in her back. Call it a mystery or a miracle, but the disc healed and the dislike dissolved into love. We were married the following fall.

Our relationship was very typical. Very normal. I set out to conquer the world and she set out to populate it. That was the way God had ordained things, wasn't it?

It's only looking back that I realize the changes. Gradually, bit by bit, Bev came out of her shell, and gradually, bit by bit, I discovered my humanity.

A few of the assumptions about our relationship and her identity began to be challenged. Just a little.

She studied theology on the side, and earned a degree, magna cum laude. The significance of that escaped me at the time.

Bev is now an ordained minister. Winfield is her first full-time pastorate. It was here that our kids learned what it was like to be a P.K. (Preacher's Kid) and I learned what it was like to be a P.S. (Preacher's Spouse or Post Script, take

·your pick.)

A clergyman moving and bringing a wife along seemed normal. But a woman arriving with a husband in tow gave rise to a bit of speculation about "what's wrong with him?" And besides, what do you do with a minister's husband?

A pastor's wife would obviously play the piano, join the women's group and bake pies for the bazaar. But a husband?

What possible use could there be for such a creature?

Where do babies come from?

Actually, I'm disgustingly normal. It's just that I have a talent for finding myself in slightly unusual circumstances.

Like being married to a minister. Never having been married to anyone else, it's hard to compare. But it feels normal. In fact, I'd even be prepared to say we're in love. After 25 years!

Even after all this time some of our relatives still haven't got it all straight. We got a long letter asking in terribly polite language, how to address a letter to a couple when she is a "Rev." and he is nothing in particular.

"It's easy," I say. "Just send it to 'Rev. & Mr.' or 'Mr. & Rev.' Whatever you like. How about just 'Bev and Ralph?'"

But when you tell people that, you can almost see their mental computers overloading.

Sometimes people shuffle from one foot to another trying to ask me what it's like being married to a lady minister.

"I was married to her long before she was a minister," I usually say. "When she became a minister it didn't seem to make any difference. Same girl."

That doesn't seem to be enough for them, so I usually add, "Lots of guys have their wives preach at them but mine is specially trained." It's slightly sexist but it seems to lower their anxiety a bit.

You never get these strange questions from people in our congregation. To them she's simply a person. The confusion comes when some unwary stranger looks the name up in the phone book and gives us a ring.

"May I speak to the Reverend please." Of course it's always one of our teenagers who has answered the phone, so the receiver gets handed to Bev.

"Hello?" she says.

"Oh, sorry," says the voice at the other end. "I wanted to speak to Mr. Milton."

The phone gets handed to me.

"Hello?"

"Ah ... listen Reverend. Me and my girl, we was thinkin' of gettin' married, eh, and ..."

"Just a minute, you want to speak to my wife." I hand the phone back to Bev.

"Hello".

"Ah ... is this the Reverend?"

"Yes."

"Like, are you the minister?" The voice is sounding incredulous.

"Yes, can I help you?" Bev says cheerfully.

People who haven't been to church since they dropped out of Sunday school seem to have strange out-dated ideas of what it's all about, and they get themselves into the silliest corners. Imagine this at a service club meeting.

"What did you say your name was?" We were standing around trying to recover from an after-lunch speaker.

"Milton, Ralph."

"Don't I know you from somewhere? The name sounds familiar."

"Possibly. More likely you know my wife. She's the minister at one of the churches here in town."

There's a long silence while that sinks in. Then trying to say something, he sputters, "Ah...do you have a family?" He blushes deep red, and I wonder why.

"Yes, we have four children."

The man is obviously surprised. "My God," he

mutters. Then clearing his threat, he recovers slightly and says, "I mean, a clergyman having babies...ah...I mean..." The man is completely flustered.

"Relax," I say as kindly as possible. "Clergymen seldom have babies, but clergywomen do, and they do exactly what other women do in order to get them."

There's a pause, then a giggle, finally a laugh. "Isn't it amazing the assumptions we make when we don't stop to think. Well, anyway, can I buy you a cup of coffee or something? Being married to a minister, you must need something to steady your nerves now and again."

"Amen," I say as we head down the corridor to the coffee shop. "In fact anybody married to anybody needs something for their nerves now and again."

Faking it

Crossing over the great divide from B.C. into Alberta last fall, we smelled oil the moment we crossed the border. It might have been the huge flatulent semi-trailer just ahead.

Bev and I had been invited to do an anniversary event for St. Andrew's, our church home in Calgary for nine years. It was wonderful seeing so many old friends. Like me, they were all greyer, balder and paunchier.

It was also frustrating, because we didn't really get to talk to any of them. At least not enough to get beyond the little verbal games we play with each other.

"Well, hi there!"

He's a great big tall fellow, with a face I vaguely remember. I decide to fake it.

"Hi! Good to see you again."

"Gee, it's been a long time. How's ah....how's everybody at home?"

Now I know he's faking it too. He doesn't know who I am either. It's comforting.

Suddenly a light goes on in my head, and I remember a younger, thinner face with more hair on top. We were together on the music committee. But everything else including the name eludes me. It's time to eat humble pie.

"Look, I've been talking to so many old friends today, and I'm having trouble pulling names out of my head. A sure sign of senility."

"John," he says. "John Gower. And I have the same trouble, all the time." Now I have him at a disadvantage. Should I be kind, or make him squirm. I decide to be kind.

"In that case, I'll tell you who I am, so you won't have to ask. I'm Ralph Milton."

"Oh, I remembered your name all right," he fibs. "It's your wife's name I couldn't dig up."

"It's Bev."

The blighter! Now he's got me squirming. I have no idea if he's even married, much less the name of his wife. I decide to use his ploy.

"So how's everybody at home?" I ask.

"Oh, just fine. Fine. Marg has decided to go back to work, now that the kids are pretty well grown."

Bingo! I have her name. And I also know there's a family.

"Got any pictures of the kids?" That's a dangerous question. Some people will promptly haul out a wallet full of badly focused snapshots and you're there for an hour. This time I'm lucky.

"I can do better than that." He grabs my arm and hauls me over to the side of the room where a gaggle of teenagers is playing the kind of games teenagers play with each other.

"Cindy and Elaine. Do you remember Mr. Milton?" They don't, and find the question embarrassing.

But I remember. It's the two freckle faced skinny-as-a-rail gigglers I taught in Sunday School years ago.

"Holy smoke! Are you sure? Last time I saw you, you were only this high." That embarrasses them even more. So I make my exit. "Well, you're obviously busy.

But it's good seeing you."

This time I take John's arm, and move him away from the teenagers. "They don't want to talk to old geezers like me, John. But it sure brings back memories. They were such bright and cheeful kids, as I remember. How are they making out?"

I see the flicker of pain in his eyes and hear the slight catch in his voice before he says, "Fine. They're doing just fine."

"Watching teenagers grow into adults is easily the toughest thing I've ever had to do."

"Yeah." I can see a tear struggling for birth in his eyes. "Look, I gotta run. Marg'll be waiting. Nice seeing you again."

He's gone. And I stand there wondering why it's so hard for men to really talk to each other.

Kissing a dirty ashtray

I was about two or three, I think, when my cousin Pete blew cigarette smoke into my ear to stop an ear ache.

That made me sick to my stomach. When I stopped throwing up, I still had the earache.

You'd think that would have burned itself into my psyche enough so I would never have started smoking.

From my venerable perspective of 49 years, it doesn't make much sense. But at the age of 17 I sat on the front stoop of my boarding house with a package of Players Mild and taught myself how to smoke.

I still remember the awful taste, and wondering why people did this. But all my friends thought it was cool, and that was all the convincing I needed.

In fact, I was quite convinced I'd never impress any girls at all, unless I could light up with the macho flair of Humphrey Bogart. So I practised in front of a mirror.

It wasn't too many years later, when I was thoroughly hooked on the weed, that a girl I was going out with told me, "kissing a man who smokes is like making love to a dirty ashtray." The romance didn't last.

Of course I resolved right then and there to quit. By that time I knew I didn't enjoy smoking. I smoked only because I had this deep down craving that almost drove me bananas when I didn't.

I resolved to quit all over again several years later when I saw a little sign that read:

<u>When you inhale the smoke
from your cigarette,
you are exercising
your rights.
When you exhale
the smoke
from your cigarette,
you are
violating mine.
Therefore,
smokers are requested
not to exhale.</u>

I quit hundreds of times. Sometimes for five minutes, sometimes for days. Tobacco, the scientists tell us, is more addictive than booze or hard drugs. And nobody knows how addictive it is until you try to quit after puffing yourself to death for 20 years.

When I saw my father-in-law dying from emphysema, after a lifetime of puffing away, I knew I was going to quit for real.

Quitting was awful!

The craving gnaws away at your innards for days and days and weeks on end. And just when it starts to go away, someone comes along and lights up beside you, and you start all over again.

It wasn't until a year later, when I was sitting in a waiting room, that I knew I had the habit beaten. There was a pack of smokes and matches on the table beside me. Nobody was around. I simply had to try a cigarette.

One puff, and I headed for the bathroom to rinse out my mouth. It tasted like smoldering leaves, which shouldn't be surprising, I guess.

Come to think of it, that's what cousin Pete always smelled like.

Come to think of it, cousin Pete was a bachelor all his life.

Flip, tug and pat

I heard it on the radio. "You can tell whether a married couple is liberated by who makes the bed." Ever since, I've been trying to figure out how knowing who makes the bed tells you that.

Being a naturally sloppy person, I prefer to leave the bed unmade and simply shut the door. It seems logical, since I'm simply going to mess it up again in a few hours.

But if we're going to make it, and Bev insists that we do, then it would seem that the person most capable of making it, should do it. Right? It's only logical.

And Bev, after all, was trained as a young girl to

make beds. With a flip and a tug and a pat she can have
the whole thing done in no time flat.

I don't manage quite as well. In fact, whenever I
flip something, it flips in the wrong direction. If I
tug, it pulls out whatever I've tucked in on the other
side, and my pats are mostly a desperate last-ditch
attempt to flatten the lumps underneath.

So it would seem reasonable that Bev should always
make the bed.

However, she seems to feel that since I messed up
at least 50% of it, I should straighten out at least
50% of it. And I have to grudgingly admit there is a
kind of logic about that.

"OK honey, you make your side, and I'll make
mine," I said nobly.

It's a great theory. It doesn't work.

At least not if she makes her side at a different
time than you're making your side, because whoever does
it last unmakes the side that was made first. (Do you
understand that, or should I run through it again?)

It does work however, if you do it at the same
time, and develop a bit of intricate team-work so that
you both tug the sheets just the right amount to pull
them tight without yanking them out of the partner's
hand. Flip, tug, pat and in about one half of two
shakes you can have it done. Actually kind of fun and
satisfying.

Maybe real liberation is doing it together.

IV
A man's a man for a' that

I'm proud of my nose

It's genetic. I got it from my father. Like me, he had a petite nose when he was a boy, but it grew faster than he did.

It's taken me 49 years but I can now say for sure that I am proud of my nose and no longer sensitive about it.

(And you stop snickering, or I'll plow you!)

I'm proud of my nose because I've discovered a host of great and famous people who had large noses. Well, four anyway.

Remember General de Gaulle? It took a lot of gall to come over to Quebec and shout freedom slogans. De Gaulle had nerve, even if he didn't have much diplomacy. And that's what people always tell me too. "Ralph," they say, "you've got a lot of nerve".

Then there was Cyrano de Bergerac. He wasn't a real person actually, just a character in a play who got to impale people on his sword while he recited poetry. He didn't get the girl in the end (it was some handsome klutz that got her), but he did have some good lines, especially about his nose. Like, "when it bleeds, there's the Red Sea!"

Jimmy Durante made a fortune from his nose. Have you ever heard of anyone with a small nose making any money out of it? And Barbara Streisand. If she had married Pierre Trudeau, she could have been really famous and written a book and everything.

Obviously a big nose is more valuable than a small one, as any racehorse will tell you.

Think of the advantages. When I catch a cold I can walk in the dark and see perfectly well. It's like having a built-in miner's light. It's handy but it keeps Bev awake nights. That, and the fact that when I blow it she usually winds up on the floor.

Once when I was walking home from work I sneezed a couple of times. It broke a window in a nearby home and several mothers ran out to get their kids off the street.

In the days before I kicked the smoking habit I could puff a cigar in the shower. Not that I ever did--I hate cigars--but it was comforting to know it was possible. And my moustache never gets wet. That's good too. You know how frizzy a moustache gets in the moisture.

My nose is one of the reasons I wear a beard. It's an artistic consideration, you see. I am widely regarded as being terribly handsome. I have been mistaken for Kenny Rogers, though not when I was singing. And somebody once said I reminded him of the Yogi Maharishi, though not while I was talking philosophy.

There is one minor flaw. My nose preceds me by a fair distance so a touch of fuzz on the lip and chin creates a bit of balance, as it were, and my profile isn't quite so much like the east coast of North America.

Large noses are a sign of intelligence and character. In a recent nation-wide survey of six people, the four with the largest noses were able to answer more skill-testing questions among them than the two with small noses.

A nose like mine is hard to forget about. Over the years, I've come to think of it as one of God's special blessings. Egotists like me need that sort of thing to keep us humble.

At last.
A cure for the
common cold

This is national "feel sorry for Ralph" week. I am having my semi-annual cold, and I am miserable. Cards, letters and money should be sent to me c/o Wood Lake Books. Especially money.

My colds come in two stages. During stage one, my throat feels like I just drank a half-pint of battery acid. Or coin-machine coffee. Same thing, actually.

During the second stage, my throat feels fine but the whole business heads up into my eyes and nose, so that my face looks like two maraschino cherries and a plum floating in a glass of buttermilk.

My nose drips enough water to irrigate the whole town, and after the 5,997th blow even those extra super soft tissues feel like Richard Nixon's five o'clock shadow.

A cold wouldn't be so bad for me if I were an ordinary mortal. But I am unique. My kids call it weird.

You see, somewhere in my genetic past lurks an Australian anteater. Or at least a camel. That's why Mom Nature endowed me with an inverted washtub for a nose. Actually, it's quite beautiful, once you get used to it. An acquired taste.

Normally it just hangs there, a contented conglomeration of flab and cartilage through which I manage, somehow, to breathe. Its interior is well lined with shrubbery which has to be mowed about once a month. This allows me to strain out gnats, earwigs, and geese flying south.

But when I have a cold the whole thing bursts into bloom. It comes alive with an irridescent glow that lights up the countryside, a beacon of hope to the weary night-time traveller. When I drive a car at night people pull over to the curb expecting a speeding ticket. I may be miserable with a cold but my nose is having a fantastic time.

This may be an appropriate time to offer the world my favorite cold remedy. It's actually the product of years of research and experimentation.

An uncle of mine tried it. He died, but his cold was definitely cured.

Here's the remedy. Pour yourself one very tall glass of very hot rum (this is for medicinal purposes so its OK), find two aspirin and all the blankets you can collect. Sit on the edge of the bed.

That's important; I mean about sitting on the edge of the bed. In fact, you'd be well advised to do anything else that requires mobility before you proceed. Like going to the bathroom. Or making out your will.

O.K. Are you ready? Pop the two aspirin in your mouth and down the entire glass of rum, chug-a-lug. Get under the covers. Quick. You have four seconds.

Stay under the covers and sweat for eight hours.

This cure comes with a money back guarantee. We guarantee that you will not feel the same after the treatment as you did before.

But beware of aftereffects. My cousin tried it. Now she goes around kissing any stranger with the sniffles.

Relativity
and the art of cross-country skiing

"If you can walk, you can cross-country ski." That's what the man said, sitting right in my living room.

We had some friends over on New Year's Day.

"I'd really like to do that some day," I said with my usual effervescence. "I just haven't gotten around to buying the equipment."

"We have some equipment you can borrow," said another friend.

If I'd had any sense I would have popped up to re-fill the coffee cups or go to the bathroom or have a heart attack.

"Say, that's great," I said. "Why not call me some time when you're going skiing."

"How about tomorrow afternoon?"

The dreaded afternoon turned out to be a beautiful day in spite of my night-long supplications pleading for a blizzard or a sudden thaw. Bright, clear sunshine over a light new snow. It was glorious. It would have been hard not to enjoy almost anything outdoors that day, though I was determined to try.

My friend and instructor loped along effortlessly through the orchard, stopping to wait every 50 feet or so, while I did the Politician's Strut: one slide forward, a red-faced puff, and two slides backward.

I should explain here that I had never been on skis before in my life, except on one occasion. I was twelve, when I travelled 20 feet downhill on a pair of borrowed skis, coming to a most undignified halt against a row of garbage cans. That moment came back to haunt me as we reached the crest of a hill.

My kind instructor showed me how to do the downhill. "Point the tips of your skis together," he said, "and if you're still going too fast just sit down and use your bottom to stop."

I had some reservations about using my behind as a brake. After all I use my derriere daily. Sitting is one of my favorite postures, next to lying down.

But I knew I had no choice as I went hurtling down a cliff that would have given Podborski goose pimples. My ski tips refused to point together at the toes. I had visions of my left foot going right and my right foot going left, and me winding up as a human pretzel act in a travelling circus.

So I let out a blood-curdling scream that sterilized the entire orchard for three seasons. My instructor stood to one side, and I went streaking by at 800 miles an hour.

You may well ask how it is possible to reach a speed of 800 miles an hour in the space of 40 feet. Peter Einstein's Theory of Relativity. It says that the speed at which you are travelling is directly proportional to your utter panic multiplied by your incompetence.

I did survive my adventure just as I manage to survive almost anything. Even Christmas. And after the kindly ministrations of my instructor, who carefully dusted off the south end of my anatomy that I had been dragging through the snow, and then offered me a cup of hot tea and plenty of sympathy, I managed to get home all by myself.

I have made a solemn promise to my "maximus gluteus" never to put it in such dire peril again.

But why am I sitting here looking at ski equipment in the catalogue?

Sweep, turkey!

Once in the dear dead days beyond recall, when in the west, winter followed fall, one of those poor hapless Scottish settlers Lord Selkirk brought to southern Manitoba looked out of the tiny window in a sod hut at a raging prairie blizzard, and in a fine Scottish burr said, "Yeach...what a drag."

Life in southern Manitoba during the winter was a bit tedious in those days (it still is). There was literally nothing to do. The livestock all froze solid on October 1st, and so didn't need feeding again till they thawed on March 30th.

"Why don't you go curling?" said his wife.

"Don't know any girls!" he grumped.

"Curling, not girling, you twit," said his wife sympathetically in her soft highland brogue. "The pond is frozen. Here's a left-over haggis you can put a handle on. It's better than granite anytime. Go find your buddy Wullie McCrimmond and get out of here. Yer driving me bananas."

That's how the canny Scots brought curling from a loch near the wee hoose mang the heather to the pond near the out hoos mang the muskeg. Why they played it in Scotland in the first place is one of those eternal mysteries which, along with their love of bagpipes, will never be understood by anyone born south of Manchester.

Just in case you're not familiar with the game, here's how it works. On one end of a long skating rink one of the players has a big 50 pound rock. Why they made it that heavy is part of the mystery. They could as easily have made it 5 pounds and out of plastic. Maybe they needed something hard to work off their aggression after playing bagpipes all day.

The player slides the rock slowly down the ice. Sliding it too fast is a waste of time because it just ends up in Saskatchewan. The other players, not having anything to do, run alongside the rock, and whenever they get a bit bored, they sweep the ice in front of the rock with silly little brooms, the kind witches ride.

The skip doesn't skip. The skip just stands there and yells. If the players are just running alongside doing nothing, the skip hollers SWEEEEEEEP! If they are busily sweeping, then it's proper to holler WHOOOOO-OAAA! Whoa is something that works equally well with horses and curlers.

There is a myth, by the way, that the sweeping makes some difference to the speed at which the rock is sliding. Actually, it's a ploy dreamed up by the canny Scots who didn't want to buy fuel to heat the rink, and encouraged sweeping to keep the curlers warm.

The proper way to slide that rock is with the 3-N technique. Nose, navel and knee. Some people have a problem with that style of delivery, because their navel is somewhat closer to the ice than either nose or knee. In my case the nose is the problem. It tends to cut a furrow in the ice if I don't keep my head up.

Before the player throws the rock, the skip hollers instructions. "Don't be heavy! Don't be light! Don't be wide! Don't be narrow!" Having all that helpful advice the player can then, without fail, deliver as per instructions.

Curling is Canada's great national sport. If it hadn't been for curling, all three of our prairie provinces would have been abandoned in 1935 by settlers bored batty by eight months of winter. As it is, there are only two kinds of people living in Manitoba. Those who curl and those who go to Florida for the winter.

Curling gave us Canadians our great call to action; our national slogan. The Americans have "Nuke 'em!" The English have, "Be British!" The French have "Ooo-la-la!" The Russians have "Nyet!"

We have the greatest battle cry of all: "Sweep, turkey!"

The natural look in monks

I once went to a barber who was an Edmonton Eskimo fan. I don't have anything against barbers rooting for the Edmonton Eskimos. If you've been looking at people's dandruff all day, you certainly need something to get your mind off your work.

But this particular barber was not just a fan; he was a fanatic. He talked and talked about Warren Moon till I wondered if he had become a Moonie. But I didn't really mind too much until he held up the mirror.

"Yikes", I yelled. "Give me a saffron robe and I could join the Hare Krishnas!"

"Don't you like it?" he asked.

"Don't you think you cut it kinda short?"

"Yeah. I guess. Maybe I got talkin' too much."

I changed barbers.

The next one had a brother-in-law who did toupees. He had a very interesting way of bringing up the subject.

"Them guys that have money, they sure spend it."

"Huh?" It wasn't a very intelligent response but it wasn't the easiest statement to respond to.

"Like Elton John. He had one of them deals where they take the hair from his chest and transplant it on his head."

"Oh."

"And, like, Frank Sinatra, eh? He wears a toupee."

"Good for him."

"I have this brother-in-law who makes toupees so natural you don't even notice nothin'."

"Good for him."

"You want me to give you his phone number?"

"No."

"He's cheap. Like, he don't charge much."

"No thanks. You see, my friends have a pool going at the office to see whether the last hair to fall out will be grey or black."

This barber gave a very nice haircut, but I had to

switch again because we moved to Winfield, and driving back to Calgary for a haircut would have been inconvenient.

That's when I met Karen. Bev had gone to Karen to have her hair frizzed, and suggested I go to get my hair cut.

"Real men don't go to beauty parlors," I said.

Bev gave me one of those withering "Come off it, Ralph!" looks. I went.

Karen, I discovered, gives good haircuts. But that's not why I go back there. Karen is good looking, but that's not why I go back there, either.

Karen has a very wholesome attitude toward balding men.

"Hey, a neat bald spot you got there," she said.

"Thanks," I said. "I kind of like it too. I think it makes me look like a monk."

"A what?"

"Monk. A male nun. People who aren't ministers or priests but make a career out of working for God. You know, the guys in the middle ages who walked around in long brown dressing gowns with a rope around the middle. They'd shave a circle on the top of their heads because they figured that looked religious."

"Well you're not a monk. Why do you want to look like one?"

"I am, kind of."

"I thought you wrote magazine articles and books?"

"I do. But it's all religious stuff."

"Is there any money in that?"

"No."

"You're nuts, you know. Why don't you write Harlequin Romances? That's where the money is."

"No thanks," I said. "I'd rather be a monk."

"What a drag!"

"No, it isn't. At least not if you're a Protestant monk. You get to do some things that Catholic monks can't."

"Like what?" Karen asked innocently.

"Never mind. Give me a haircut?"

"I could sort of tidy your bald spot up a bit. Clean out the fuzz in the middle and make it a nice tidy round circle."

"No thanks, Karen," I said. "The natural look is in, even for monks."

A pain in the neck

The Chinese used to practise foot binding. We still practise neck binding. And ours is supposed to be an advanced culture.

I mean why, for heaven's sake, would anyone ever wear a tie? Why would any half-way rational intelligent male voluntarily subject himself to this ancient instrument of torture? Maybe we've cut the circulation off from our heads for so long, our brains have shrivelled like a Japanese orange in January. We can't think any more.

A tie has absolutely no function except to clean eye glasses and it doesn't even do that well. It just smears the muck around. It makes about as much sense as those grenade loops we used to have on trench coats. Maybe even less, because the guy with the trench coat could at least carry grenades if he happened to be a revolutionary. What can you do with a tie?

It doesn't impress anybody. Nobody even notices, unless you wear one so bilious you can hear it a block away. Then people just pretend they don't know you.

My Dad used to be a teacher in southern Manitoba. He got 45 ties as gifts every Christmas. Every student gave Dad a tie. Either that or shaving lotion that smelled like kerosene. The shaving lotion hit the slop pail. Our hog, who got the slops, would wear a silly grin for the whole twelve days of Christmas.

Dad felt he had a moral obligation to wear every tie at least once during the school year. And how that man would suffer. Especially about the 40th school day after Christmas when he was down to the most vile half dozen. But always, with mother muttering little words of encouragement, he would bind the vulgar thing about his neck and trudge off to school, his overcoat done up to his ears. And the kids used to wonder why March was so miserable in Manitoba.

Back to the point. Why should a piece of rag, knotted at the throat, be respectable dress for a man? It's not natural. In most parts of the world men don't wear ties. In the Philippines we wore a pretty shirt called a "barong tagalog" which was sticky and uncomfortable, but at least it wasn't a pain in the neck.

Here in Lake Country, we can spot foreigners from Kelowna and Vancouver a mile away because they wear ties. For us, going formal means putting on a clean pair of jeans.

At this point I want to inject a little "research", just to show you this is a high-class scholarly book.

It was the Croatian army that started the whole thing. They were feeling a bit giddy after beating the Turks 10-2 in a war, back in the 17th century. They started wearing the flowing "cravats" which the French army copied because they didn't have any more taste than the school kids in southern Manitoba. And over the centuries there have been thousands of pointless variations on things to wear around the neck, from stocks through string ties.

I was with a guy in Toronto once who couldn't get into a restaurant because he wasn't wearing a tie. He went into the men's toilet, pulled a lace from his shoe, put it around his turtleneck sweater, and they let him in.

The only males allowed into restaurants like that (of which, thankfully, there are few) without a tie are clergy. That is, they can get in without a tie if they wear an even more ridiculous alternative, a stiff Roman collar. The clerical collar (for the benefit of lay people) is a miniature neck brace, which not only cuts off circulation to the head but makes it impossible to nod, thus keeping the poor preacher from saying "yes" to anything that might be fun.

And ours is supposed to be an advanced culture!

V
God laughs too

When I grow up

As far back as I can remember, people were asking me, "What are you going to be when you grow up?"

As a kid, I probably had some ideas about being a cowboy or a pilot, or something. I can't remember. I can't ever remember wanting to be anything in particular, nor for that matter can I remember wanting to grow up.

Many years later, when I was about 45, they rephrased the question. "What are your career objectives?"

I didn't know the answer then, and I don't know it now. What I do know is that through most of my adult life both Bev and I have felt a gentle hand in the small of the back gently pushing us to do things we'd never thought of on our own.

Just after we were married, I found myself flailing about not wanting to do my work at a small radio station in Trail B.C. I was a "jock" running one of the very first open-line shows in Canada--a bit of history my teenage daughters find hard to believe.

We pushed at all sorts of doors looking for a way into something more meaningful. They slammed shut in our faces. Finally, we decided just to hunker down and stay where we were. There wasn't any option.

We'd no sooner done that, when a door we'd never dreamed of swung open. Missionary work in the Philippines, where we spent five fantastic years.

The pattern repeated itself when we moved to New York, when we went to Calgary, and again coming to the Okanagan. Each time we've banged at doors that wouldn't open. As soon as we gave up and decide to stay put, something turns up that isn't quite what we were thinking of, but exactly what we needed.

That's why we now find ourselves living in the Okanagan, a valley we've enjoyed on summer vacation dozens of times, but never dreamed of living in.

That is how I came to be a publisher, and work in partnership with Jim Taylor, a man I have come to love as a brother, but whom I also respect as a very fine editor and writer.

The distant sound of laughter

As miracles go, it doesn't rank with the parting of the Red Sea or changing water into wine. But do you remember the broken biffy aboard one of the first U.S. space shuttle flights? I think it was a miracle. A very small one, but a miracle still.

Or maybe it's a very small heresy. You tell me.

Every once in a while, when humans, either individually or collectively, get swelled heads, something happens that makes them aware of their humanity. The American establishment is certainly very proud of the technological accomplishment involved in the space shuttle. Maybe they should be. But it seemed to be a bit of divine poetic justice when those superbly trained astronauts in a billion dollar craft had to contend with a busted biffy.

"God has put down the mighty from their thrones!" said Mary in the Magnificat (Luke 1: 52). The mighty astronauts were put down from their thrones, so to speak, while the whole world giggled. I'll bet God giggled too.

A few years ago, after I'd been boasting to Bev about a new promotion, my older daughter (who had been listening with very mild interest) walked up behind my chair, ran her finger around the edge of my bald spot, and said, "Dad, you've got a hole in your head." I don't think she was trying to bring me back down to earth, though she did. Again, I think God had a chuckle over it. In fact, I think maybe that's why God planned teenage daughters.

"An audio-visual expert from New York," the man called me. It was at a big mission conference in Chicago. We were in one of those big old churches, the kind with the long centre aisle slanting down to the front, the kind brides love to walk down. We were to see a film, but the projectionist didn't show up. The chap in charge of the program asked me if I could run a projector.

"A piece of cake," I said. "Sure."

Hundreds of people had gathered and were waiting. The church was full. To fill time while I was threading the projector, the man went up to the pulpit and started saying how grateful they were to have the "audio visual expert from New York" to help them out. He used that phrase several times. And I'd be lying if I said I didn't enjoy it.

Now, you know that little toggle thing on the front reel of a movie projector, the one that holds the full roll of film in place? Guess what I forgot?

The lights went off, the projector came on, and the front roll of film flipped off with a great clatter and unrolled all the way down the long, sloping aisle to the front.

I turned the projector off. The lights came on again just in time to reveal a red-faced audio visual expert from New York winding up the film from the front of the church to the back.

Following the film, there was to be a closing meditation. The scripture? You guessed it. Mary's poem, from Luke. "God has put down the mighty from their thrones...."

If you were attending a Bible Society dinner at the Mennonite Church in Winnipeg back in 1961, you would have heard me make a speech, about how the printed word was passe', and books as such would be unknown in a decade. I thought I was prophetic. A few others must have thought so too, because the speech was printed in several magazines.

Now, more than two decades later, this publisher and writer of books can hear the distant but distinct sound of laughter.

Say something in cobol

"So!" I said to Mark, my eldest son on his latest visit home from the University. "What are they teaching you in college?"

"Not much." My son is always ready to share his innermost thoughts with me.

"You gotta be learning something," I said. "It's

costing enough."

"I'm learning languages."

"French? German? Russian?" I asked.

"No, Fortran and Cobol."

"How interesting," I said, not wanting to appear dumb. "Say something in Cobol."

It only took twenty minutes to discover that Fortran and Cobol are computer languages, and that you don't talk them, you write them in strange little symbols and words that don't resemble anything anywhere.

That was a long time ago of course. Now I have my own computer and I'm very suave and sophisticated about it all. For instance, whenever I meet someone with a new home computer I can assume an air of knowledgeability and ask, "How many 'K' does it have?"

"Thirty-two," comes the breathless response. "But it has two disk drives!"

"Mine has 64K and four drives," I say, trying not to sound too superior. Then I quickly divert the conversation to something else before they discover I haven't the faintest idea what a 'K' is. I don't know what a 'bit' is either, though I've had it explained at least twenty times.

The problem is that a computer is based on a kind of straight-line logic that doesn't make any sense. For instance, when you crank the thing up in the morning it wants to know the date (I have no idea why) and you have to write it like this; 01/05/1984. If you do it even a teeny bit different, such as use a capital "O" instead of a zero, it yells "Bad Response" over and over at you until you fix it.

So I talk to my partner Jim. He has a computer just like mine. His is called Abigail. Mine is called Wolfgang.

"Does Abigail insult you like Wolfgang insults me?" I ask.

"Yes," says Jim. "Computers have rotten manners. And twice when I have been right in the middle of a page, I accidentally hit the wrong combination of keys and got a flashing signal that says, 'There is no such page'. And it turns out to be right. There was, but now there isn't. It's erased the whole thing!"

"I thought computers were supposed to be smart."

"Well if adaptability to change is a measure of intelligence, then Abigail is an idiot," Jim said. "So far, I have done all the adapting."

"Still, I wouldn't trade Wolfgang for anything," I said.

"Neither would I," says Jim.

Now I'm trying to convert Bev. I figure she needs a computer on which to write her sermons.

Her method is to plan months ahead what she is going to talk about on a particular Sunday. Then everytime she gets an idea or some new information on the subject she clips it to the sermon outline. A week beforehand, she types it out.

Except that she never likes her first draft, or her second, or even her third. She keeps writing in corrections and additions and amendments in between the lines and up and down the sides until on Sunday morning it looks as if she's interpreting chicken entrails.

"I haven't the foggiest idea how those things work," she objects. "And frankly, I'm not interested. Besides, I haven't got time to spend six months learning a silly computer."

Bev has been intimidated by the "computer talk" she hears from time to time. Computer buffs are like car enthusiasts. They like to impress each other by all the words they know.

"I've been readin' the specs on the TW9-98ZX-5," they'll say, "but the random access parallel interface of the megabyte migrain won't match the multi-dimensional graphics matrix of the hexadecimal conversion in the DKD-H998-D. What do you think?"

Well, I don't.

At least not like that. I figure it this way. I can drive a car anywhere I want without having any idea what goes on under the hood. "Bev," I say to her, "Wolfgang is no harder to learn to operate than our Volkswagen. And probably easier to learn than that new sewing machine of yours that does everything except make toast."

She's not convinced, but I am.

I've been using Wolfgang's Word Processor for a couple of years churning out hundreds of letters, dozens of magazine articles and two books. It's the best invention since sliced bread though it does tend to bring on a mild case of verbal diarrhea. (Jim warns that it is contagious!)

There is one bit of computer lingo I do understand. GI=GO. That stands for Garbage In equals Garbage Out.

This book was written on a computer.

The ghost of Christmas past

An interesting thing about the Okanagan. You never know for sure if there'll be snow for Christmas. Where I grew up in southern Manitoba, we knew. You could be sure about certain things like death, taxes and snow at Christmas.

Okanagan Christmases can be that wet grey-green monochrome that gives some people arthritis and others the "blahs". But when it snows it's beautiful. There's a sparkling glory to the place that sings right out of the trees at you.

Snow and Christmas go together for me. When there is no snow I miss it terribly. I'm writing this on Friday, December 18th, and looking out the window, hoping the brightness will last the week. We'll have the whole family home, and there'll be all those good familiar things that make Christmas such a rich and meaningful time. You get that warm feeling in the pit of the stomach that can't be cured by chewing Tums.

It's hard for me to imagine Christmas without snow and tinsel and family. But I don't have to imagine. I can remember. Christmas 1961.

Bev and I were young and full of vim and vinegar. When you're 23 you're ready to conquer the world. We were going to start with the Philippine Islands where we'd been sent as missionaries.

We arrived early in December, a month before most of our baggage, so we had nothing whatever to decorate the house for the Christmas season. There wasn't a pine tree within a thousand miles.

It simply didn't feel like Christmas. And we had two small kids in tow! If anything should make you feel Christmasy, it's kids. I remember thinking that at least their little bottoms looked Christmasy. They were a brilliant scarlet with diaper rash from the heat.

Filipinos solve the problem of diaper rash very logically. They remove the diaper. Kids run around with a shirt but no bottom. Everyone is happier.

The interesting thing about tropical heat is that at first you enjoy it. You go to the beach and get sunburned in December and think it's fantastic. The second week you wish it would cool down just a mite.

The third week, you wilt. Any starch or ambition you had is wiped away with the sweat that flows constantly. Eventually, you start checking the mirror to see if you've turned into a prune.

We hit Christmas on that third week. And as if we weren't feeling low enough, I came down with an unmentionable illness.

(Well, I guess you might as well know. Most of us are adults here. I had to go into the hospital to have a hemorrhoid removed. There. I've told you. Don't let it go any farther. Promise?)

They let me out two days before Christmas. Things like sitting, standing, walking and lying down were difficult. Other than that, I was fine.

On December 24th it still wasn't Christmas for us. We gathered some shells at the beach and painted them pretty colors, just for a bit of decoration. It helped a little but not much.

We bought a few gifts for the kids because most of the real Christmas presents for them and for us were in that baggage that hadn't arrived.

There is something terribly, desperately lonely about having Christmas among strangers in a strange place. There seemed to be nothing we could do to make it feel like Christmas. We didn't have a thing to make it look like Christmas, or smell or taste like Christmas. In the local market, they didn't even know what a turkey was.

All we had was each other.

And our faith.

So we held hands and walked through the humid night to church that Christmas Eve. And there, with strangers whom we recognized as future friends, we heard again the ancient ageless story. And we found Christmas.

Or maybe it found us.

VI

The world traveller

Just in time...just

I still don't believe it. Deep down inside the dark recesses of my subconscious, a small squeaky voice keeps saying, "Airplanes can't fly. It's impossible."

I have logged thousands of air miles, flown to 30 different countries on everything from a Piper Cub to a 747. And if you ever travelled with me, you'd immediately recognize the jaunty air of a seasoned traveller.

That squeaky little voice doesn't communicate with my face or my hands or feet, or anything that you can see. But it's got a hot line direct to my stomach. And at the slightest provocation, it picks up the phone and yells, "Ha! You're going to crash. I told you so."

I have a friend who is a pilot. He assures me that flying is absolutely the safest form of travel. Statistically he's right. I know that. But emotionally, I'm with my mother who declared that if God had intended us to fly, we'd have sprouted wings.

My faith in technology and pilots is pretty fragile, and they'd never get me on to one of those things if I didn't believe in miracles. Flying, for me, is a miracle. I know you can explain it all with principles of physics, but that doesn't make it any less a miracle.

There's another miracle I need very badly in order for me to fly. That's the miracle of knowing that my death in an airline crash would not be the end of my life.

It all started back in 1961. Bev and I and Mark, who was just over a year old, were on our way back to Trail, B.C., after having been accepted by our Church mission board to go to the Philippines as missionaries. We were on one of those awful DC-3's, the Model T of the airways, trying to land at the Castlegar airport. It was only the second time I had ever been on an aircraft. I was not enjoying myself.

Castlegar airport is located at the bottom of a canyon and the planes have to dive in like Spitfires on a strafing run in order to get to the runway.

It had been a bumpy flight. Bev, who is prone to motion sickness anyway, was very pregnant with Kari, and concentrating on the open end of the barf bag. I had Mark standing on my lap. He was facing backwards over my shoulder.

Just as we came in for a landing, Mark began to get a bit agitated. As I pulled him around, he let fly all over the man behind us and caught the lady across the aisle. The poor man sitting in front of us got it in the neck. By the time I had him around facing me, he was finished.

As the plane came down, the fumes came up. The contents of a small boy's stomach are not too helpful in the badly ventilated cabin of a small plane. A dozen people reached for the barf bags, while the distinguished business people on three sides of us mopped away with whatever was available.

As the craft finally made its "complete and full stop in front of the terminal building", I muttered some hasty apologies, and we ran.

Bev, Mark and I came out of it smelling like a rose. I wish I could have said as much for our fellow passengers.

It seems like so long ago. I have probably flown a thousand aircraft since then, but I still don't enjoy it.

They don't fly those DC-3s much any more. Nowadays they use those flying boxcars which I like even less. They're a dozen seats wide, and the airlines have it arranged so that you always get the window seat on a cloudy day or a night flight. You get an aisle seat on clear sunny days.

Usually they serve the rubber chicken and plastic vegetables just before you land so there's no time to have a second cup of coffee. This time they barely left the ground before the stewardii came down the aisle with that little box on wheels in which they keep the food trays. It is not a good time to get up and try to squeeze past them to the biffy.

So I sat still. Or at least, I tried to sit as still as it's possible to sit under the circumstance, though I noticed I finished my meal twenty minutes before the people beside me.

Several eternities later, my bladder threatening an explosion that would have brought the craft down in flames, they got those little carts out of the aisle. I climbed over all the nice people sitting beside me, and with as much dignity as I could muster, rushed to the back of the plane.

A dozen people were in the line ahead of me.

Being the unflappable world traveller, I stood

calmly in line, looking with casual interest at all those around me, and whistled a few verses of "Nearer My God to Thee."

Up until that time, the flight had been smooth and quiet. Not a ripple. But at a point where I simply couldn't contain myself a moment longer and I finally reached the head of the line and slid myself into that tiny little excuse for a toilet, we hit one. A big one. A great big huge vast airpocket.

I don't know how long I stood there unzipped and feeling utterly frustrated. Don't ask me how it works, but something about that airpocket had removed all desire, sensation, need. Whatever.

Meanwhile the little sign was flashing, "Return to your seats" and being a good little boy, I returned. The "Fasten seat belts" sign was on as I climbed over the laps of those very nice people back to my window seat where I could look at the clouds outside.

Would you believe what happened as soon as I sat down? No, I didn't disgrace myself. But the sensation that first big airpocket had taken away, the smaller airpockets were now stimulating. And the "Fasten seat belts" sign was still on. And on. Everytime we hit another bump, my seat belt squeezed my bladder as if it were kneading bread.

Now it may be your experience that people trying to get off airplanes are sometimes a little pushy. I just want you to know there are occasions when people pushing to get off the plane in a great hurry have something on their minds that you don't know about.

I claim the world record for the 100 yard sprint down the corridor of the Toronto airport, where I reached the men's room. Just in time.

Just.

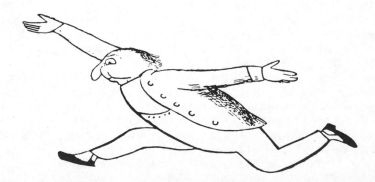

So far from Toronto

The problem with living in the Okanagan Valley is that it's so far from Toronto where everything happens.

And it costs a bundle to fly there. Half a bundle if you take the "El Cheapo Special," also known as "the cattle car."

You fly in an airborne auditorium called a 747, big enough to play the Grey Cup. The thorax of this monster whale is for "regular" passengers, the plutocrats who pay full fare. They get meals, free earphones and a well-rehearsed word of cheer from the stewdardii.

Those of us travelling to church meetings feel ultra guilty if we don't take the cattle car. So we allow ourselves to be herded into the bowels of this behemoth.

I draw seat 44E. I wonder why that man smirks when he sticks it on my boarding pass. Soon I stop wondering.

Seat 44E is exactly 23.47 inches from the five-foot wide movie screen. That's not bad, until the movie comes on.

I don't have three bucks for earphones, and be-sides the movie is something about horses. I'll improve my mind by reading a trashy novel.

Have you ever tried to read a book with horses gal-loping back and forth 23.47 inches from your nose? It can't be done.

So I watch the silly movie, and it's just as bor-ing as I thought it would be, especially since I can't hear any sound. Not even hoofbeats. And at 23.47 in-ches, I can't see properly out of either the tops or the bottoms of my bifocals.

Soon my eyes hurt, so I decide to go to sleep. Did you know that if you have a movie screen 23.47 inches from your nose, you can see the light flickering through your eyelids? Or do I just have extra thin eyelids?

Finally we arrive, sore eyes, galloping horses and all. The flight attendant puts on her plastic smile, stands at the door, looking relieved at our leaving.

Toronto is hot. Sticky. Smelly. My clothes stick and my eyes burn. The air is so bad, I try not to inhale.

My cab driver and another have a yelling match over who saw me first. Finally, the other cabbie slams his door in a huff, and mine takes me careening down a six lane highway, flipping from one lane to another as he vents his spleen through the accelerator.

I survive. But I expect the cabbie to die of heart failure in five years.

What is it about the eyes of people in downtown Toronto? Are they just tired?

Or is it a deep unnamed bitterness; a jaded hurt of people who have plenty of pleasure but so little joy? Is that what I see in the hollow eyes of a man my age staring absently at a photo of sagging nakedness on a movie marquee that promises everything and nothing?

Flying home in our giant airship, we push upward through the acrid smog and clouds; the angry air shakes our wings demanding that we stay to share the city's misery.

But the will to home is strong and we break through. The flight attendant, I think, may be smiling with her eyes. There is sunshine through my window and I know that above clouds there is always a clear blue sky.

The great thing about living here: it's so far from Toronto.

It never snows in Vancouver

It was the best show in years. Vancouver in the snow is funnier than rubber toothpicks.

You notice the cars first. They go careening around in fantastic fishtails, back wheels spinning in a slow-motion ballet that ends abruptly with the crunch of fenders and tinkle of glass.

It's not that Vancouver drivers don't know how to

drive in the snow. Most of them are prairie transplants. They learned snow survival in kindergarten.

Once they move to Disneyland North, they renounce
snow. It becomes an article of faith. They simply do
not believe that it can snow in Vancouver. And what you
believe can be a stronger reality than what you
experience.

Snow tires are banned on the coast because they re-
fuse to admit even the possibility of needing them. Neither is it legal to carry any of the paraphernalia--
like snow-scrapers.

I watched a self-important junior executive in pin-
stripe suit, tan trench coat and blow-dried hair scrap-
ing the ice from the windshield of his TransAm with a
pocket comb. Several unsuccessful minutes later he
switched to a nailfile. He finally managed to make a
peep hole three inches across, before he walked around
to get into his car, and stepped into six inches of
slush with his shiny loafers.

That got him even more annoyed, so he slammed the
door, which of course brought the snow from the top of
the windshield sliding over his peep hole. He jumped
out, stepped in the slush again, cleaned his windshield, stepped in the slush a third time as he got
back in, started the engine of his brand new bright red
TransAm, and threw it into reverse.

While he had been busy cleaning his windshield and
wetting his feet, a big grey Brinks truck had parked
its solid steel hulk two feet behind the TransAm.

It was not a good day for self-important junior
executives.

Coastal cities have bylaws against owning snow
shovels. People either leave the snow, assuming it
doesn't exist or will melt in fifteen minutes, or they
try shovelling it off with a garden trowel. But snow,
as the rest of the world knows, gets packed down into
very slick ice.

Which makes it also not good for clothes-conscious
ladies. Especially those wearing high fashion boots
with long spike heels and thin leather soles.

There was one lady who must have been a ballerina
or an acrobatic dancer when she wasn't running the
boardroom in one of those tall glass boxes they call
office buildings. She was running for a bus, and
almost made it. Then quite spontaneously she demon-
strated for all of us a spectacular sequence of pirou-
ettes and half-gainers that sent skirt and purse and

cape and gloves and herself in as many directions. Immediately she was surrounded by a male chorus of chivalrous swains who slid and swooped as they tried to pick her and her wardrobe off the street. It was a little like the dance sequence in an old Astaire/Rogers movie.

That night I told all this to my son, who has now lived three years out there in Lotus Land; my own son who lived 10 years in Calgary and Winnipeg.

"Dad," he said, "it never snows in Vancouver!"

Bombs and gifts

It was a flight from New York to Toronto. A bit bumpy. Just enough to make you aware of your stomach.

Then, BAM! And a flash of brilliant light!

There were screams and gasps. Then nothing. We just kept flying right along as if everything was quite normal. Eventually (it seemed like ten minutes later) a laconic pilot spoke over the loudspeaker.

"You may have noticed a slight noise and bit of a flash a few moments ago," he drolled. "Nothing to worry about. We were hit by lightning".

That's all.

Almost everyone has their favorite airline horror story. Mine involves taking a flight on FAST Airlines from Manila to Dumaguete City in the Philippines. I took it because it was cheap. Missionary salaries didn't allow much for luxuries.

Ten minutes out of Manila, the rickety DC-3 did a sharp U-turn and landed us back where we started. The passengers were herded out of the plane, to swelter in the tropical heat with only the meagre shade of the plane's wing to protect us from the blazing sun.

A mechanic eventually sauntered out of a nearby hanger, and began tinkering with the engine. Two miserable hours later, we were all herded back on board.

Including the mechanic. I wondered whether I was reassured by that or not.

The mechanic sat near the window watching the engine as it sputtered and spewed oil over the tropical rain forest. At each stop, he got out and tinkered.

Finally we landed at Iloilo. "All those passengers travelling beyond Dumaguete should disembark at this point," we were told. Since I was going to Dumaguete, I stayed on. One passenger. One mechanic and the crew.

And the mechanic had shifted to the other side of the plane. I wondered why.

As the engines strained and rattled over the fetid, unexplored jungle covering the mountains of Negros Island, I asked the mechanic, "Why are we not going beyond Dumaguete?"

"Because," he said, "we are having trouble with the other engine now too."

I'm always interested in what happens to me when I catch a glimpse of my own death. I remember wondering why I wasn't afraid; why I was so certain we were not going to crash. At the same time, I wondered what death in the rain forest would be like.

When we were struck by lightning on that flight from New York to Toronto, the first thing that came into my head was, "Well, if I'm going to die, I'm going to enjoy it."

That's all! And I'm still trying to figure out what I meant.

I was flying out of Kelowna recently on an assignment for a church magazine. The seatbelt sign had just gone off, and I was gazing at the mountain where loggers had cut huge bald spots along the ridges. The flight attendant had just started smiling her way up and down the aisle with plastic cups of lukewarm coffee, when the pilot suddenly stood the plane on its wingtip in a quick U-turn back to Kelowna, which didn't help keep the coffee in the cups or in our stomachs.

"Ladies and gentlemen," said a very flustered voice on the loudspeaker, "we're going back to Kelowna, and...and...as soon as the plane hits the ground...I mean as soon as the aircraft has landed...get out as fast as you can and don't try to take any luggage or anything with you and for goodness sake, KEEP CALM!"

It was the longest trip home I've ever been on. The flight attendants kept walking up and down the aisle smiling broadly through clenched teeth. Nobody was talking.

Me? I wasn't frightened. I wasn't worried. Not a bit of it.

I was terrified!!! Pure, utter unvarnished scared. I could feel my heart banging away against my ribs. I was panting as if I had just run a mile, and squeezing the armrest till it yelped.

It was a bomb scare. Some poor demented soul had phoned in a threat. And while most of us were sure it was a hoax, we were still glad the airline was taking it seriously.

A couple of hours later, after a thorough search of everything, we were on our way again. And then I had time to think a little--to reflect on the feelings I'd experienced when that aircraft was rushing home to safety.

I had been afraid all right. But after about five minutes, the terror gave way to a kind of peacefulness, and I found myself wondering if this really was the end of my life.

I was terrified of dying, but I found I wasn't afraid of death. In the middle of that fear, I found peace.

Looking back over my life, I knew it had at least been worth living. And a quiet, wordless prayer formed inside me. It was a prayer for those I would leave behind. It was gratitude for the life I would leave. And thanks for the life I knew would follow.

Even fear brings its gifts.

VII
Down home

Tea on tap

Greatness is spawned in the pit of adversity. For weeks, I've been worrying about our water supply, which every spring turns a dark brindle brown. "Hot and cold running crud", grumbled my neighbour.

But I've had a revelation. A vision. It all came to me after working out in the hot sun all day. I was sitting in the tub when, like Archimedes, I shouted "Eureka!"

Do you know why people around here are so healthy? Do you know why my bald spot is actually getting smaller? No, my head is not shrinking.

Do you know why apples grow so big? It has nothing to do with the fertilizer.

Do you know why people look so tanned? It has nothing to do with the sun.

Do you know why our churches are bursting with enthusiastic, dedicated Christians? It's not the preaching.

Tea! Yes, believe it, dear friends, believe it!

Herbal tea! According to the Oxford Dictionary (and who knows more about tea than the Dons of Oxford?) tea is an "infusion or decoction (I don't know what that means either) of leaves as beverage; infusion, etc. of leaves of plants or other substance."

What all that means, I think, is that if you soak or boil leaves or any herb in water, and some of it dissolves, you've got tea. By that definition coffee is tea.

Anyway, I have it on good authority that the color of our water comes from the pine needles in the hills above Beaver Lake where our community gets its water. The water oozing through all that piney mulch turns out to be tea, and that makes us the only community I know of with tea on tap.

We water our orchards and gardens with it. We bathe in it. We drink it. That is why we are such wonderful people!

This could bring untold spiritual and material blessings to our community. We'll bottle it and sell it at the fruit stands and supermarkets. Heck, we'll sell it all over the world.

After all, if Perrier can sell foul-tasting well water, we can sell our tea. With three spoons of sugar, half a cup of lemon and a touch of garlic salt, it doesn't taste half bad.

And it'll create a housing boom. The price of real estate will sky-rocket.

Churches will spring up on every corner because people baptized in our tea are 99 and 44/100% more devout than people baptized in plain water. They also put more money in the collection plate. It actually averages 20% more, the baptists running highest at 50% because they immerse.

The United and Catholics, being very ecologically minded and careful to conserve water, only sprinkle so they run lowest at 7.8%. Mennonite increases are 22% because they pour.

Everybody will want to move here.

One of my friends, a charismatic real estate salesperson tries hard to express his faith through his work. He leads his clients gently into the bathroom, lifts the lid to the biffy, points to the deep amber liquid and says very softly, "See. You too could be baptized in that."

The blessings of an Okanagan summer

Everybody has to do their bit to help solve the world's problems. One Sunday, after Bev had preached a sermon about reaching out to neighbors in distress, I decided that my friend Fred, who owed me 300 dollars, might be in distress and need a bit of counselling.

"Hello, Fred?"

"Yeah."

"Fred, this is Ralph. When you going to come and pick up that Chevy you bought from me?"

"I been trying to get over there, Ralph, but I ain't had time. I'll try gettin over in the next week or so."

"You havin' second thoughts? I mean, I gave you a good price. Real good. Three hundred bucks is a steal.

"I need it, Ralph. We was going to use it to pull our trailer. The Volkswagen wouldn't haul a 24 foot trailer no more. I think it needs work on the motor. Anyway, we was thinking of taking the kids for a bit of vacation this summer. We didn't manage to get away last summer. We thought maybe this summer ..."

"Visitors, Fred?"

"Yeah. Visitors, Ralph."

"Bad, eh?"

"We thought we might get away last weekend. My second-cousin from Ogema, Saskatchewan, had been here for two weeks with her seven kids, and my step-sister-in-law from Grass River, Manitoba, had been here for six days. We finally talked them into going to see some relatives in Penticton. And we just got them out the driveway, when a whole carload arrived from Balzac, Alberta. Then an hour later my half-brother's third cousin from Eyebrow, Saskatchewan, drove up with a whole stationwagon full.."

"You must have a close-knit family, Fred."

"Heck, no. We never saw them people when we was livin' in Piapot, Saskatchewan. I thought the only relatives we had lived in Penticton. We used to go see them every summer for a couple of weeks."

"You got a pool, Fred?"

"Yeah."

"And a boat?"

"Yeah. So?"

"I'm comin' around with the backhoe to fill up your pool, and I'll take the boat away when I leave."

"Look, I was up till three last night helping Edith get food ready. I'm not in the mood for jokes."

"I'm not joking. An act of mercy. Save you from suffocation, bankruptcy and premature old age. You're a nice guy, Fred. I don't want to see you go under like all the rest of them Alberta and Saskatchewan transplants."

"But Ralph! I like swimming and boating. I..."

"It's not a matter of likes, Fred. It's survival. Either that or charge admission. I'll set up one of

them toll gates on your front driveway. Twenty bucks a
day. Thirty bucks with meals. You'll either get rich
or run out of relatives fast."
"But Ralph..."
"The other thing you gotta do is get religion."
"What do you mean, get religion. I go to church
every Sunday."
"Not that kind of religion, Fred. Some sect. The
kind that hand out pamphlets and magazines. You give
one to every relative that comes in the door and tell
them that the prayer meeting starts in an hour."
"Ralph, listen, I..."
"It's survival, Fred. Survival!"

The fine art of small talk

British Columbia is simply Saskatchewan with wrinkles.
Winfield is Watrus West.
Most of the people who live in BC come from Saskatchewan. They're refugees, in a sense, running away from
people who can't talk about anything except the
weather.
So they come streaming across the Rockies like
lemmings, hoping that not only will it be warmer but
that somebody will be able to start a conversation with
something other than, "Boy, this is some weather we're
having."
What they don't realize is that everybody else
here is a refugee from Saskatchewan (or Alberta which
is just as worse) and has never had any experience talking about anything besides the weather either. After
all, a Saskatchewan farmer who has moved to BC is still
a Saskatchewan farmer.
But at least the Saskwatchers can talk about the
weather. Alberterers forgot how to do that when Peter
Lougheed came along and preached the Gospel according
to Mammon. Now all they can do is count money, which is
a useful skill but doesn't make for much social
interchange.
It's a problem for the churches, especially the
clergy.

Theological schools and seminaries on the prairies never tell their student clergy how to move a conversation from the weather to spiritual matters. So two years after they are sent to their first congregation in Saskatchewan, the young clergy seem to hear a "call" to Alberta. In Alberta they talk about money, except they call it "stewardship" because it sounds more religious. When they see retirement coming they hear another call to BC.

Graduates of west coast schools, all of whom go there from the prairies hoping to talk about something besides the weather, are sent back to Saskatchewan for "the cure." After all, you wouldn't want them going around trying to start meaningful conversations, especially about Christian faith and how you live it.

There are of course, a few native British Columbians still surviving, but they are an endangered species. A small herd was spotted recently in the hills behind Kelowna.

They're not much better as conversationalists. After they've discussed the love-life of a coddling moth or the mating habits of the salmon, they run dry. It should be said to their credit however, that when the temperature hits 10 degrees below freezing they do blow their noses most expressively.

Here and there, you find a few foreign missionaries from the far east (Manitoba), where the art of conversation blossoms. In Manitoba, everyone is either Hutterite, Scottish, French, Ukrainian, Jewish, Metis, Indian or Mennonite (like me).

Nobody speaks English. Eaton's store on Portage Avenue sounds like the Full Gospel Businessmen going full bore speaking in tongues. It makes for great, non-threatening conversation, because all you do is smile and nod your head and wait for the other person to take a breath. Then you start.

No one understands a thing. And everybody is happy.

Stark naked on a tractor

In the heart of every overweight suburbanite male lies the conviction that he could be a good farmer. If he wanted to. So when John Towgood's tractor needed to be moved 10 km from Winfield to Oyama, I jumped at the chance.

Memories of childhood days, riding on my old Uncle Henry's tractor, the one with the steel lugs and the huge flywheel, came flowing back into my mind. Driving a tractor from Winfield to Oyama on a snowy winter day would be great fun. A breeze.

A breeze all right. A freezing breeze that zipped through all my ultra warm clothing and left me wondering if I was driving that tractor stark naked.

"Be sure to dress warm," John had said. "It's mighty cold on that tractor."

So I dug out my long-johns, the ones I used to wear in Calgary. Can underwear shrink from being left in the bottom dresser drawer? Or is it possible that I've grown six inches since I turned 40?

At any rate, my long-johns were now short-johns. They came just below my knee and looked like knickerbockers you'd wear to a fashionable cricket match. And the longest warm socks I could find pulled up just above my ankles. Which left a nice big gap for the breeze to bite me.

By the time I finished driving that tractor to Oyama, John had to pry me off the tractor with a crowbar. "Why didn't you tell me riding a tractor was going to be cold?" I chattered.

John also hadn't told me a few other things about tractors. They don't have springs and shock absorbers and the other civilized amenities of modern travel. So hurtling along the road at 5 miles an hour, I hit a pot hole.

Bang! The shock reverberated through each of my vertebrae up my spine and hit me with a wallop on the back of my neck.

I don't know how long it was before I came to. It might have been hours. It might have been 1/87th of a second. But the tractor held true on its course, moving straight ahead.

That's another thing John didn't tell me about

tractors. They don't have front wheels.

Those round things on the front with the tires? They're just decoration. The wheel you hold in your hands and turn from side? That's to amuse the kids when you bring them along.

Unless the ground is absolutely bone dry, those front things have no bearing whatever on the trajectory of the tractor. When I was driving from Winfield to Oyama, the snow kept falling and the road was slippery. The big rubber lugs on the back kept the machine moving straight ahead. You could turn the steering wheel any-which direction, and it made not a bit of difference.

How then, you may well ask, do you get a tractor from Winfield to Oyama, when the road between these two cities is anything but straight?

You use the brakes.

Of course it doesn't make sense. You don't turn things with brakes. You stop things with brakes. And it's all very hard to understand until you see that name "Massey" painted on the side of the machine. The Massey's were an Ontario family that turned out Governors General and Ottawa functionaires. As a side-line, they made tractors.

Steering with brakes instead of a steering wheel is typical of the way Ottawa solves the problems of western farmers. It only makes sense if you've never tried it.

It also explains something else I've wondered about. To turn the tractor, you hit the left brake to turn left, and the right brake to turn right, which is logical, except that if you press it just a teeny bit too hard, it does a complete 360 and lands you upside down in the ditch.

That's why there are so few old farmers.

Too good for TV

They packed the hall on Sunday night. Every chair we had was set up, and people stood around the edges. It was a celebration of Christmas and a celebration of community.

The Elementary School choir got us off to a happy start with a set of rollicking songs. Tanya Jones blushed and Chris Warrington boomed their way through solo parts. And by the time they were finished we all knew exactly why we had come.

Then the Grade Three choir lisped their way through a clutch of carols, and the Junior Choir from the church bounced us through a couple of snappy Christmas hymns.

Diane Friesen directed with everything she was, from her toe nails to her hair follicles. It showed in her shoulders, in her hips and the sway of her head. I kept wishing I could see her face. The kids could, and her enthusiasm reflected in their eyes.

There were no spectators. They were our kids, our friends, our family, our neighbors. And even though we weren't on stage, emotionally at least, we were participants.

We felt even worse than Tony did when his music fell off the piano and he had to start all over again. And when the Grade Three choir got a bit mixed up in their story of Silent Night we struggled as hard as they to get the thing together again.

That's what community means. Feeling the pain when things go wrong, and shouting together when things go right. And celebrating both.

There wasn't a thing in that program that was good enough for television. In fact, if you squeezed it through the wires and transistors of a television transmission, all the juice would have been lost and you'd have had nothing but a badly done amateur hour.

Come to think of it though, the evening was really much too good for television.

We'd been brought together by the love that's there in the middle of Christmas. And though we came from different religious traditions, or none at all, we were all there because we cared about somebody else; somebody who was playing or singing or reading.

And caring about somebody else is somewhere near the heart of Christmas.

VIII
The wonderful world of weeds

The joy of gardening

There is abroad in this land a myth, a superstition, that home gardening is an easy-going, genteel, relaxing recreation, ideal for people prone to ulcers and high blood pressure. Like the myth that governments exist to serve the people, the reverse is true.

To be a successful home gardener, you need the wisdom of Solomon, the perceptions of a Sherlock Holmes, the cool of an N.H.L. goaltender, and the theatrical pizzaz of Mary Tyler Moore.

The pressure begins somewhere in January, when the icy winds blow and the snow flies, and the temperature falls out the bottom of the thermometer. That's when the seed catalogues arrive, with their full color verdance bursting from every page, seducing you into midwinter fantasies of growing orchids in your orchard and pineapples on your patio.

The photos are brilliant. The descriptions are even brillianter. They reek with promises. Each paragraph of purple prose promises a "bumper crop"; a "first rate harvest" and other superlatives, as if each seed is the ne plus ultra of seediness.

This is where your Solomon wisdom comes in. You've got to know, from years of experience, not to believe a bit of it. None. Not a word. Or as the Russians say, in a word that has much more negative power than our English "no", "Nyet".

But you still have to buy seeds, so here's where the Sherlock Holmes thing comes in. Those descriptions actually do tell you something, but not by what they say. It's by what they leave out.

Look at some tomato seed packet for instance. It tells you each plant will produce half a ton of huge red, delicious tomatoes suitable for canning, eating fresh and playing basketball. They are hardy enough to plant under the snow in fall and will be up before the crocii. But does it say anything about "the grundge"?

As every tomato grower knows, there is an unidentified plague that attacks tomato plants about the time you figure you've got the garden in shape and you can afford to go away for a weekend. Now if your seed catalogue doesn't say anything about the grundge, you can bet your last petunia that the minute you turn your back, or maybe even while you're watching (some varieties of grundge are exhibitionists), it'll turn all that red ripe fruit into sludge.

On the other hand, if the description of the tomato seed tells you about all its magnificent grundge-fighting capabilities, but says nothing about its hardiness, you know you've got a plant that keels over with the first cool breeze in August.

Even though you may be able to psych out the seed catalogue, you still need the cool of an N.H.L. goalie. In fact, that's probably the most vital characteristic of a successful gardener. You need it to fend off all the helpful advice your friends give you. Everybody in this world thinks they know everything about gardening, and if you invite anyone to come and see your backyard beauties, you'll immediately be buried in enough advice to keep your garden in humus for a decade.

A few gardeners (may their green thumbs twitch in peace) have tried to heed the wise words of friends and neighbors. They have been so frustrated by all the contradictory advice, they wound up beating their own brains with an over-ripe zucchini.

Remember the N.H.L. goalie. Never take anybody's advice. Turn all their comments aside, while nodding, and maybe even occasionally making notes. It's important that you give the appearance of listening. That may require a theatrical performance worthy of Marlon Brando.

This is terribly important. Because if you don't, you'll never be able to give advice back. And that is the greatest (and perhaps the only) joy of gardening.

The crabgrass headache remedy

The doctor jabbed his finger into the flab where my stomach muscle used to be. "That is your problem!" he said.

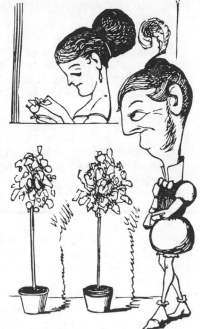

"My stomach is causing my headaches?"

"No. You're flabby. You're not getting any exercise. You love your work and you're excited about it. But that excitement gets all kinds of juices pumping from your glands, and you've got to work them out of your system. If not, they'll hit you in your weakest spot."

"Meaning my head."

"So I can pump you full of pills or you can do something hard and physical and cure your headaches that way. Take your pick."

I didn't like the doctor's prescription, because physically I'm lazy. But I didn't like having my head torn off by tension headaches every two weeks either.

I'm the same weight now as I was when I was 16, more or less (mostly more). The only thing that's changed is the distribution and the texture.

Muscle takes up less space than flab, so my 32 inch waistline is still 32 inches, but if I want to breathe I wear size 38 pants.

One of the things about a mid-life crisis is that you become aware of your body. It doesn't really feel any different. It just doesn't respond as well.

That seems to include everything from how long it takes to recover from a game of touch football, to the games you play in bed. The recyling time is longer.

Most of the people I know who are my age have decided to take up jogging. Including me.

Most of them quit after about a week. Including me.

I had a good excuse. The only good place to jog around here had a German Shepherd on one side of the road and a Doberman Pinscher on the other. Both hated joggers.

I tried swimming, but you get all wet doing that, and besides, swimming laps is even less interesting than jogging, because you have to keep your head under water most of the time. And the scenery becomes mildly monotonous after the 20th lap.

Another thing you do about the mid-point of life is to read the labels on food packages. The list of ingredients reads like a recipe for Macbeth's witches. Sugar seems to be added to everything.

And you have upsetting conversations. Like the one with a medical friend I asked about all the chemicals in foods. "The three chemicals that kill the most people are sugar, nicotine and alcohol, in that order," he said.

So if you have a concern for what you eat, a need to get some exercise, and a few vague ideas about living responsibly on a shrinking planet, the answer is gardening.

At least for the summer months it is. I could flail away at weeds and crab grass and work up a dandy sweat while getting rid of all those headache-causing juices the doctor was talking about. And half an hour of getting my back teeth loosened by the asthmatic roto-tiller is as good as three hours in the ring with a Sumo wrestler.

After the first summer in the Okanagan, I was tanned and fit and no more headaches. I also got rid of the hyper-acid stomach the Doc said was caused by the same thing; tension. So we wound up with enough V-8 juice to start a filling station, and a 46 cubic foot freezer full of frozen tomatoes I had to chop out with a pick-axe.

I had the satisfaction of knowing that I was giving my family organic vegetables, i.e. vegetables with dirt on the outside and worms on the inside. The net result was a happier, more contented Dad.

Even my spiritual life improved when I was more physically fit, which is more evidence, if more evidence is needed, that the body, mind and soul are all part of the same package. I could stay awake through sermons. When your wife is the preacher, and you are sitting in the choir for the whole congregation to watch, that is important.

However. I have a problem. While my head is going a mile a minute, physically I am lazy. When there is something non-physical to do that looks like fun, I can think of a dozen reasons why it's more important than digging the parsnips. So I'm slipping. My paunch is growing back almost as fast as the weeds in the garden.

Willpower seems harder to come by as I get older. But last fall my brother had a heart attack. And he isn't that much older than I. So I give myself a little lecture. Time to put first things first, Ralph baby.

Besides, I enjoy the gardening, once I get myself out there. And when the harvest starts to come in, and I walk into the garden to pick that first fresh tomato, and eat it, still warm from the sun, right there in the garden, I know it's worth it.

There is something powerful and good about growing your own food. It's not just the money it saves or the wholesome food it provides, though that is important.

There is a sense of being in touch with the earth; in touch with the seasons; in touch with life at a basic level; in touch with God's grand design.

And there are many times, planting the seeds or pulling the weeds, when my thoughts very naturally turn into prayer.

What kind of bull is this?

It says here on this seed package: "Requires a rich, well nourished soil, slightly acid, with plenty of humus, well drained with plenty of sunshine."

Fine, fine. The only thing I can guarantee out of all this is the bit about being well drained. My garden may not be much else, but it is well drained; a gravel pit on a hillside. It's like pouring water on a sieve. The only plants that survive are the ones with vacuum tubes on their roots to catch the drops of water on the way by. Or those with tap-roots that go 317 feet down to lake level. In other words, weeds.

As for the sunshine, that's beyond my authority.

Having a gravel pit for a garden, I decided to do something about the "rich, well nourished" part. Last spring I hauled in seven back-breaking loads of manure from my cousin Jack's cows. It was good manure. Except

that Jack's cows don't
digest seeds.

Those seeds soak
in that manure all the
way through the cow and
for a month or so out
on Jack's back forty.
When they hit my garden
..... vaaaaaroooooommmm!
Nourished by the manure
and by a good soaking
of the nice brown water
we get out of our taps,
they turned my garden
into an Indonesian
jungle.

If I had been a really proper gardener I would
have gone to one of those gardening stores and bought
bags full of steer manure, all nicely sterilized and
weed free. But I'm suspicious.

For instance, how do they know that's only <u>steer</u>
manure? Can they really guarantee there's no cow,
bull, or heifer manure mixed in there? How do they
keep it separate? Do they have over-sized outhouses
marked, "His", "Hers" and "Its"?

If I am going to pay five or ten dollars a bag for
steer manure, I want to be sure it's steer manure. I
don't want to get it home and discover it's a bunch of
bull.

Last fall I got smart. "No more of Jack's seedy
manure", I said to myself. So I used green manure--
winter rye! I planted it all over my garden.

Winter rye grows very well. The book says you
plant it in the garden in the fall, and in the spring-
time you turn it under and it provides rich mulch for
your soil and helps suppress weeds in the process.

They were right. It grows very well, particularly
if you have a mild winter. So now I have a garden that
looks like the African savanna after the rainy season.
I tried cutting down the winter rye with my lawn mower,
but it started sounding like a third-rate movie star doing a death scene in a fourth-rate flick. My roto-
tiller wouldn't till. It wouldn't even roto.

Does anyone know how much it costs to pave a whole
yard with green concrete?

How to succeed at gardening without ever touching a hoe

Every year at this time the competition rages. There are no declared winners and no prizes, but the warfare is fierce and battle bloody. It's called the "Have-you-got-your-garden-in-yet?" contest. There are no referees, but everybody knows how to keep score.

The rules are simple. Go up to a known gardener and say in your most friendly manner, "Hi, Mary! Lovely day isn't it? Got your garden in yet?"

At that point Mary will try desperately to find an excuse. "Oh well", she'll mumble, "we've had so much company, and I fell and broke two of my legs and I had the flu".

It's no use. In this game no excuse is valid. You have your garden in or you don't have it in. If you don't your penalty is to listen to the following gloat:

"Oh, that's too bad. I got my peas in three months ago and they're up and blooming. We've been eating radishes and lettuce, and I transplanted all my cabbage, and my tomatoes are ready to go into the garden but, oh dear me, I do hope it warms up enough so I can put them out before they get too big" etc., etc., etc., ad nauseum!

Mary has to stand there and take it and you get to stand there and dish it out. Them's the rules.

You see, Mary should have known better. She should never have responded with an excuse. The only way out of the competition is not to enter in the first place.

You can do that by looking very disdainful and saying, "Well, we decided we had better things to do than bend over in the hot sun all summer. So we just paid a quarter of a million (it's best if the price is very high) to cover all four acres with green carpet, the kind undertakers use when they bury people."

On the other hand, if Mary had been a professional in this game of gardening oneupmanship, she would have said, "I'm trying a new experiment this year. I'm letting all the weeds grow six feet high, then I'm going to mow them down as green manure, plant my seeds, and cover the whole business with four feet of a very special mulch I've developed. It's one part apple mush, one part shredded newspapers, one part polyunsaturated chicken manure, and one part dried Eurasian milfoil. I've gone organic, you see, and I feel this way of doing my gardening would be more ecologically responsible."

It's best if you say that sort of thing to the gardener who pours a half-ton of chemicals on everything. You get extra points for making people feel guilty, especially gardeners who grow absolutely beautiful stuff but use chemical fertilizers. Any organic gardeners worth their compost can out-guilt the chemical fertilizer people 6 to 1 with their green thumbs tied behind their backs.

Gardening offers such rich rewards!

The law of the jungle

Ah, sweet autumn. The breath of harvest fills the nights; the morns are crisp with promised frost.

It is joyous indeed! Yes, joyous to walk through the autumn orchards. Fa la la, and that sort of thing.

But please, don't walk anywhere near my garden. I'm not ashamed of it or anything. I'm mortified. And the neighbours are starting to talk.

Mom nature and my own natural lazy streak have done me in. And the only safe way to enter my garden is with a machete knife and a Burmese guide.

It all began when I read a subversive magazine called Harrowsmith. An article said the easiest way to compost was just to throw the stuff right on the garden and not bother with compost piles and all that work. "Direct composting", they called it.

"Aha!" I said to myself. "Now you're talking my language". (I've always taken the view that ambition and the tendency to work hard are flaws of character that can be overcome. Over the years I've managed to refine my personality to the point of utter sloth.)

I really went for direct composting. All last year the weeds that got pulled, usually when they were

nicely mature and full of
seeds, just got plowed into
the garden.

And kitchen compost
too. Just throw it in and
dig it under, said the article. It's easy.

Did you know that
squash, pumpkin, zucchini
and cucumber have an average
of 8,999,878.5 seeds each?
And did you know that 8,999,
877.5 of those seeds will
germinate if you throw them
in the garden with the kitchen compost?

Furthermore, did you know that couch grass seed
will germinate before, after, and during the hot, cold,
wet and dry seasons? In fact, better than anything,
anytime.

So last spring I planted carrots. They didn't
grow. But the grass and the squash did. I planted carrots again, and they didn't grow again. But the grass
and the squash did. I planted carrots a third time and
they didn't grow a third time. But the grass and the
squash did.

Lately, I have been looking in recipe books for
things to do with squash and grass. I found some
things you can do with squash. Most of them involve adding everything imaginable so it doesn't taste like
squash.

So far I haven't found a thing to do with grass.
At least nothing that's legal.

But I'm just going to have to do something about
the jungle in the back yard. Last week one of the
neighbours reported to the local paper that she'd seen
a huge hairy creature with big feet crashing through
the underbrush.

I called to her, "It's only me!"
But she'd already fainted.

Apple picking
for beginners

> Apples in spring
> Are a wonderful thing,
> But apples in fall
> Are no fun at all.

The first problem when you decide to go picking is to find the orchardist (that's a fancy name for a fruit farmer). To do this you wander all over the orchard yelling your head off for half an hour till you find yourself back where you started.

He'll be there. And since you are a beginner, he will assign you to the biggest tree in the place, the one planted by his greatgrandfather, who also built the 45 foot three-legged ladder he gives you.

Then you are fitted with a canvas and steel contraption that's half straight-jacket and half garbage pail. When you strap it on you look like a cross between an overweight kangaroo and a paunchy cow puncher.

Telling yourself that you are more brain than brawn, you decide to do the apples at the top first, since they would be the hardest. With gargantuan effort you move that frail tripod up to the tree. And you climb. And you climb.

When finally you reach the rarified atmosphere at the top, you tell yourself that it's simply the lack of oxygen, not the ladder, that gives you the sensation of swaying in the breeze. So reaching out bravely to pick the first succulent fruit, you discover that every single apple is out of reach.

Undaunted, you make your way down the ladder, push it right into the middle of the tree and proceed upward again. This time your way is blocked by a huge limb that refuses to be circumnavigated. Down you go again to reposition the ladder. A third time to the top. And though there's a touch of twinge in your knees, you have it. Success!

Like a trimphant flag-pole sitter swaying in the

damp breeze, you see a thousand apples all within easy
reach. Eagerly you begin.

"A piece of cake", you say to yourself triumphant-
ly, as you see how quickly and easily the kangaroo
pouch fills.

Time to go down and empty the bag. But wait. No
one mentioned to you that whereas one apple weighs not
much, a pouch full of apples weighs a ton or so. Furthermore, the pouch is draped conveniently over the top
of the ladder.

You survey the situation. Your choices are three,
all of them questionable.

1) Lift the pouch up over the top of the ladder.
One step up and the ladder sways from side to side like
Trudeau at election time.

2) Pull the bag around the side. Fine, except
that makes the ladder lean drunkenly and you can see
yourself impaled on a spiked branch that threatens you
from below.

3) Remove the bag from your body, lift it over the
ladder and carry it down. Either gravity or Krazy Glue
holds the straps to your shoulders. You can't move.
You wonder how many weeks till you'd be missed, and if
they'd ever find your body at the top of the tree. You
glance up to see if there are vultures circling
overhead.

There is only one course of action. The orchardist is nowhere in sight. Quickly you toss out apples
from your bag, till finally with superhuman effort you
can wrestle it over the offending ladder. Quickly
again you pick the bag full, being careful not to get
the ladder between you and your prosthetic belly.

Then slowly, step by trembling step, feeling like
a pregnant woman with overdue sextuplets, you feel your
way down that swaying ladder. Your knees turn to silly
putty.

An hour later, when you reach terra firma, you
want to kiss the ground, but you can't bend over while
wearing that marsupial pouch. So you mutter a short
prayer of thanks instead and empty the pouch into a
huge red bin where the apples roll around looking
lonely.

"Enough!" you say. "I will immediately enroll in
a night school course and become an undertaker's
assistant!"

The offending pouch is thrown to the ground. You
run crazily through that forest of fruit, branches and

apples battering your head at every step.

Suddenly a huge man looms up before you. It is the dreaded orchardist!

"Hi", he says. "Where you off to?"

"Just looking for the bathroom," you say casually.

"It's over there," he says, pointing in the direction from which you came.

"Oh."

Carrots are only human

They say the only way to purge your psyche of guilt is to confess all. Once you have told someone how rotten you are, you'll feel good enough about yourself to go and do it all over again. Anybody who has ever been in an "encounter group" knows that.

Well, I have a need to do a bit of confessing. I have been wracked by pangs of guilt pulsating up from my ingrown toenails and down from my dandruff. My nights have been robbed of sleep, till now I walk hollow-eyed and gaunt, down the shadowed street of my despair.

It's about those carrots. I just didn't think about it at the time. I didn't really know what I was doing. I really didn't. You've got to believe that! If I had only known, if the implications of what I was doing had occurred to me, I certainly would not have been so cold-hearted, so cruel, so perverse.

Never once did I think that sorting carrots into two piles was discrimination. I had separated those that were nice and round and firm and fully packed, from those that weren't. Then a flash of insight seared my conscience. "We live in a free country!" I thought I heard a voice saying. "We have a Bill of Rights in our constitution. Wouldn't that include carrots?"

Carrots after all, can hardly be blamed for what they are. Many of them had their sides split in childhood. Should they be eternally punished for the exuberance of youth?

After all, I was the one who overfed them. I put

down a load of good organic fertilizer that my cousin Jack gave me. My carrots just went a little overboard on it, that's all. And young carrots should be allowed to sow a few wild oats.

Some of my carrots had led perfectly fine, upright lives. They grew lean and tall.

But I stabbed the poor things with a garden fork as I untimely ripped them from their earthly womb. Can you imagine anything more heartless? I tried to tell myself I didn't do it on purpose, but after all I could have been more careful. You didn't know I was that kind of person, did you?

But wait. There is more. Having sorted the poor hapless carrots, I then condemned those pitiful misshapen roots that had suffered so much already--I condemned them to mutilation, scalding and freezing.

And to add insult to their injury, the clean upright well-shaped carrots were treated to a long languorous life of leisure in a root cellar, where they will rest in sweet repose until early next spring when we will suddenly remember that we forgot about them. Then their remains will be respectfully composted. What better after-life could any carrot crave?

Thanks for listening. I feel better just having talked to you. It's good to get it off my chest. Maybe I can sleep tonight.

I need it. Tomorrow I have to do the parsnips.

A funny faith

There's much in life that isn't funny. Horrid things happen. Look in any direction and you'll see people fighting with each other. Look in our own homes and see us fighting for our emotional, spiritual and physical lives!

There are many reasons why there's so much pain. One of them, a small one perhaps but important nevertheless, is the lack of humor.

I don't think I've ever heard a sense of humor numbered as "a gift of the spirit" in church or anywhere else. But it most surely is.

Our sense of the ridiculous has much to do with our creation in the image of God. Of all God's creatures, we're probably the only ones given the gift of laughter.

Our Reformation forebears made a big mistake when they kicked laughter out of the liturgy. Humor has plenty to do with virtues such as faith, hope and love. Humorlessness is reflected in such sins as pride, greed and envy.

Religion is a laughing matter.

And humor is a pretty religious business.

Our mouths were full of laughter
and our tongues sang aloud for joy
Psalm 126